Make Social Learning Stick!
How to Guide and Nurture Social Competence
Through Everyday Routines and Activities

Elizabeth A. Sautter, MA CCC-SLP

With Contributions From:
Kari Dunn Buron, MsEd, Author of *The Incredible 5-Point Scale*
Leah Kuypers, MAEd, OTR/L, Author of *The Zones of Regulation*
Emily Rubin, MS, CCC-SLP, Coauthor of the SCERTS Model®
Sarah Ward, MS, CCC-SLP, Speaker and expert in executive functioning
Michelle Garcia Winner, MA, CCC-SLP, Creator of the Social Thinking® framework, author and speaker
Pamela Wolfberg, PhD, Author of *Play and Imagination in Children With Autism* and creator of Integrated Play Groups

APC
PUBLISHING
P.O. Box 23173
Shawnee Mission, Kansas 66283-0173
www.aapcpublishing.net

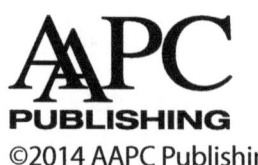

©2014 AAPC Publishing
P.O. Box 23173
Shawnee Mission, Kansas 66283-0173
www.aapcpublishing.net

Publisher's Cataloging-in-Publication

Sautter, Elizabeth.

Make social learning stick! : how to guide and nurture social competence through everyday routines and activities / Elizabeth A. Sautter. -- Shawnee Mission, Kan. : AAPC Publishing, c2014.

p. ; cm.

ISBN: 978-1-937473-83-9
LCCN: 2014930459
Includes bibliographical references.
Summary: A series of activities parents can easily fit into everyday routines as a way to help children gain and improve social competence. Arranged around three major themes: at home, in the community, and holidays and special events.--Publisher.

1. Social skills in children. 2. Social interaction in children. 3. Interpersonal communication in children. 4. Interpersonal relations in children. 5. Children--Behavior modification. 6. Children with autism spectrum disorders--Behavior modification. 7. Children--Life skills guides. I. Title.

BF723.S62 S28 2014
155.4/182--dc23   1402

This book is designed in Myriad Pro.

Interior Art: ©Lorelyn Medina; thinkstockphotos.com

Printed in the United States of America.

Contents

Acknowledgments

Many people have influenced the development of this book and the ideas presented.

A big thank-you to my business partner, Hillary Kissack, for her support and encouragement over the years. To all of the amazing therapists and staff that I am fortunate to work with at Communication Works in Oakland, California, for sharing their creativity, experiences, passion, and brilliant minds. To all of the patient parents and professionals I have partnered with to support the amazing and talented children whom I have worked with. To my colleague and dear friend, Terri Rossman, for her inspiration and continuous belief in me. To Kari Dunn Buron, Leah Kuypers, Emily Rubin, Sarah Ward, Michelle Garcia Winner, and Pamela Wolfberg for their contributions. And lastly, to my parents, for cheering me on; to my husband for his patience and love; and to my two energetic, sweet boys for keeping me on my toes, letting me practice therapy strategies with them, and forgiving me for not being a perfect mom.

Introduction

It's recess time for Johnny's fourth-grade class, and the kids run gleefully to different parts of the playground with the exception of Johnny, who sighs and then sits down on a bench and pulls a book out of his backpack. In the past, he tried to join in when a group of boys talked about movies or video games, but he always seemed to say the wrong thing. Were the other boys making fun of him? He wasn't sure. And when he approached the kids playing tag, they always told him he had to be "it," and that was no fun.

So Johnny pretends that he prefers to sit on the bench and read, even though he is feeling rejected by his peers and confused about what to do. At lunchtime, he also sits alone, and he rarely gets invited on play dates or to birthday parties. Some mornings he tells his parents he is too sick to go to school. His parents see how lonely Johnny is but don't know how to help.

The importance of *social competence*, a term that has been used to describe social success or the ability to achieve social goals, cannot be overstated. It plays a major role in developing and maintaining relationships, academic achievement, working in small groups, and eventually in holding a job (Blair, 2002; Bodrova & Leong, 2005). Our world is filled with social situations that we have to navigate by knowing when and what to say or how to act around others. This can be a struggle for those who are not hard wired to pick up on social cues or struggle to understand how to relate to others. It can also be difficult for individuals with anxiety, attention deficits, or behavioral challenges because if you are not feeling comfortable internally, it's hard to think about the external environment – the people around you and how to relate to them.

When social goals are not met, it can have a negative effect on mental health and quality of life. But the good news is that social competence **can be taught, practiced, and improved!**

Making Sense of the Social Murkiness

It is good to be aware of other terms that are used when referring to social competence, such as social communication, social skills, social language, pragmatic language, social cognition, Social Thinking®, social learning, social intelligence, and *social regulation*. As a matter of fact, it was difficult to determine the title for this book due to all the various terms used and uncertainty about which ones readers would be familiar with. However, it was felt that *social competence* is familiar and commonly understood and *social learning* is the act of gaining social skills to become socially competent, which is what we want to "stick" with our children. A brief overview is provided to clarify what is involved; however, this book is not designed to go into deep explanations or definitions of these terms. Instead, it is designed to be a useful, hands-on guide to build awareness, to help put **social skills** into practice, and to build **competence** for functional use in everyday life.

One of the key terms that is often separated out when talking about social competence is *self-regulation*. *Self-regulation* has been defined as the ability to gain control of bodily functions, manage powerful emotions, and maintain focus and attention (Shonkoff & Phillips, 2000). This is similar to self-control, self-management, anger management, impulse control, etc. When children struggle in these areas, they are often viewed as "behavioral problems" – both at home and/or school. Since social interactions can't be avoided in life; it is important to realize that self-regulation plays a huge part in social competence and cannot be viewed separately.

To make the link between self-regulation and social competence clearer, Kuypers and Sautter (2012) suggested combining the words *social* and *regulation*.[1] They define *social regulation* as the ability to adjust our level of alertness and modify how we reveal emotions and behavior in order to achieve social goals. In other words, it is the ability to monitor and adjust internal feelings and states (both mental and physical) in order to exhibit behavior that is "appropriate" for the social situation.

This may seem simple; however, social regulation is vast and complex, and many skill areas and brain functions need to be developed and integrated to keep us socially regulated. Some of the main components involved are sensory processing, emotional regulation, language processing, pragmatic language, perspective taking/theory of mind, and executive functioning, all of which are briefly reviewed below.

Sensory processing (Ayres, 2005) refers to the way we receive and manage information from the environment through our senses, such as how we sense if a sweater is comfortable or itchy based on the sense of touch. After receiving this information, we make decisions to keep ourselves feeling comfortable. For example, if it's really bright outside, we can put sunglasses on or if it's cold, we put a sweatshirt on. When children have sensory sys-tems that are over- or under-reacting, it can be difficult for them to process sensory input and feel comfortable internally, which in turn affects how they feel and act in their social environment.

Emotional regulation refers to being able to control our emotions rather than letting them control us. Experiencing emotions is innate; however, we can regulate the timing, display, duration, and intensity of how the emotion is expressed or revealed depending on the social situation. When our emotions control us, on the other hand, we might act before thinking and do something that gets us in trouble or makes someone else upset. For example, if a child is mad about what he thinks is an unfair play in a kick ball game, he might act out physically or verbally, which in turn might get him into trouble and create a larger problem.

Language also plays a part in social regulation in that the brain has to process and understand language (**language processing**) and then use the information in a socially expected manner (**pragmatic/social language**). We have to understand the words and messages being sent as well as the context and rules for how they were sent in order to know what, when, and how to effectively communicate with others and in various settings. This involves understanding verbal (spoken) and nonverbal (facial expression and body language) communication and how we change our language/communication to adapt to the situation at hand. Knowing how to "code-switch," that is, being able to change our use of language to match the people and places around us, helps with the social use of language. For example, we know that it is okay to give a high five or a hug to a good friend whom we haven't seen in a long time who comes to the front door. However, if we gave the mail carrier who comes to the front door a hug, that would be unusual and in most cases considered "inappropriate." Similarly, most people know how to change their tone of voice and body language

---

1   The authors recognize that their definition of social regulation shares similarities with other instances of its use in the literature (see Grau & Whitebread, 2012; Patrick, 1997; Volet, Vauras, & Salonen, 2009).

when they are talking to a baby versus talking to an adult. Speaking of tone, we cannot overlook the importance of being able to understand, as well as demonstrate, emotions and messages through our voices, facial expressions, body posture, hand gestures, proximity, and all other essential nonverbal clues that are involved in communication.

We also need to be able to "step into someone's shoes" or take others' per-spective, also known as **theory of mind** (Baron-Cohen, Leslie, & Frith, 1985). This refers to the ability to think about other people and what they might be thinking or feeling and understand that their thoughts, feelings, desires, and experiences differ from our own. This is similar to what is known as social cognition which, simply put, means how we think about being social and how we think about the people we are interacting with. What do we know about them? What are their beliefs, culture, age, or feel-ings? What do we know about the place or social situation at hand? How do we learn about the social rules at a new school or job? What do we say and how do we act to keep the people around us feeling comfortable? Not only can this be very abstract and difficult, but just when we think we have a social situation figured out, it changes. For example, as children get older, they may realize that it's not "cool" to kiss their parents good-bye in public any more or sit on their lap. That is why we not only have to teach the **social skills** (the behavior) but also talk about the thinking that comes before the skills or that goes hand-in-hand with the skills.

This is what Michelle Garcia Winner, a speech-language pathologist and leading expert in the area of social cognition, refers to as **Social Thinking**®.

The Social Thinking teaching framework she developed (www.socialthinking.com) helps children become better social thinkers and social problem solvers. This emphasis on thinking provides them with the tools and strategies to bet-

ter understand their social surroundings and make the best choices in terms of what skills to use in the moment. This also involves developing a sense of how their behavior affects the thoughts of others, how others treat them and, in turn, how they feel about themselves (Winner, 2005). For example, when children are playing a game and someone gets hurt, it is expected that they think about what would make that person feel better and use social skills to show that they care about her, such as stopping what they are doing and walking towards her and asking if she is okay. This would not only show that they are caring individuals but also prompt others to have positive thoughts about them.

The idea of taking another's perspective may seem "natural" to those of us with neurotypical social development, but explaining this complex concept to individuals with social learning challenges can be difficult. One strategy Winner developed to turn this abstract concept into teach-able elements is the Four Steps of Perspective Taking (see below). These steps demonstrate that taking perspective is an active process that in-volves considering our own as well as others' thoughts and feelings within the context of the situation.

The Four Steps of Perspective Taking (Winner, 2007)

1. When you come into my space, I have a little thought about you and you have a little thought about me.
2. I think about your intentions and you think about mine. Why are you near me? What do you want from me? Is it because you are just sharing space, do you intend to talk to me, or do you intend to harm me?
3. I realize you are having thoughts about me and you realize I am having thoughts about you. We each think about what the other might be thinking.

4. I monitor and possibly modify my behavior to keep you thinking about me the way I want you to think about me. You do the same toward me. The thoughts we are having about each other are often tiny thoughts that are almost at the unconscious level. However, it is this always-present, very active thought process about the people around us that allows us to constantly regulate our behavior to make sure most people have "comfortable" thoughts about us most of the time.

Finally, **executive functioning** refers to the cognitive process required to plan and direct activities (Dawson & Guare, 2010). It involves skills for emotional and impulse control, attention, motivation, flexibility, problem solving, planning, organization, and initiating. Executive skills allow us to manage those innate emotions we experience as well as monitor our behavior and ability to have effective communicative exchanges. Ward and Jacobsen (2012) add that it involves the ability to integrate a present awareness with future anticipation (forethought) and past experience (hindsight) to develop a reasonable plan for a present action or goal. For example, if a child knows that Halloween is two weeks away and he wants to be Batman, he needs to think ahead and tell his parent very soon because he can think back and remember that in the past all of the popular costumes sold out fast. Being able to stay calm, as well as plan, organize, and initiate goals, based on hindsight and forethought, is a huge part of social competence.

Making It Stick! – Carryover of Learned Skills

Most children learn how to be "social" through their everyday environment by watching, imitating, and learning from others. However, some don't learn these skills intuitively through their social milieu. This may be due to a specific diagnosis, such as an autism spectrum disorder, lack of exposure or practice in social situations, or other reasons that delay development. Whatever the cause, we need to support children to help them move from the early stages of social development of thinking about "me" to being able to relate to others and think of "we" so they can experience the pleasure of being with others and achieving their social goals. These children need direct instruction and support. They need abstract concepts broken down, explained, and practiced. For example, if we want our children to understand what "being friendly" means, we can explain this abstract term by breaking it down, defining it, talking about ways to show friendly behavior (e.g., smile, say hello, or share a toy), and talking about how it makes others feel when we use those friendly skills. As Winner's (2005) Social Thinking® concepts teach, we can help these children understand that when we are friendly that makes people feel good and want to be around us and be our friends. That, in turn, makes us feel happy and good about our behavior and ourselves.

Another challenge is when a child learns a skill in a certain setting and fails to realize that it applies to other situations, or, conversely, that similar situations require different social skills. For example, if a child is taught that greeting others with a high five is cool at school with her peers, she can learn to give high fives on the playground or when she sees people in different environments that she is familiar and friendly with. But she also needs to learn that this gesture is most likely not cool when she greets her teacher, the principal, or the bagger at the grocery store. That is, it is important to consider the context in order to know which skills pertain to a specific social situation (Barry et al., 2003; Stewart, Carr, & LeBlanc, 2007; Vermeulen, 2013). Some children struggle to understand that while a certain learned skill, such as a high five, can be used in a variety of settings with many people, when it is used in the *unexpected* way, it can cause problems. For example, asking for a high five when the child just heard that a friend got a bad grade on a test would be unexpected and considered rude.

When skills are introduced, therefore, it's essential to make sure that the child is using them correctly, not only with her friends or at school, but also with the people she interacts with in other settings. Each social interaction is unique in terms of the skills needed to be successful, and the subtle clues to figuring out what is expected in those exchanges and relations, from second to second, can be extremely nuanced and easily missed. It's important to realize this in order to support our children's ability to use their learned social skills in a variety of environments in the most successful way.

When children learn these skills and then carry them over to their natural environment and use them across multiple settings, it is called generalization or carryover. In this book, this is what we mean by the term *make it stick.*

Parents and Professionals Working as Partners

To foster and uphold the process of generalizing skills into the daily routine, everyone in the child's life must work together and support the child on a regular basis. When the home and school teams collaborate, it results in more rapid acquisition of target behaviors and increases the likelihood that positive behavior change is maintained over time (Koegel, Matos-Fredeen, Lang, & Koegel, 2011). All members of a child's life are teachers, with the parents or primary caregivers being the most important teachers, who provide opportunities for the child to learn and generalize skills for a lifetime. Parents are usually the first on the scene, and provide the greatest influence

and strongest models. Parents must be partners with the teaching team and, as such, be ready to serve as coaches in the natural environment who guide and reinforce their child to learn and be successful.

For many years as a speech-language pathologist and social cognitive specialist, I have been influenced by and have incorporated strategies from experts in the field of social learning and self-regulation into the therapy that I provide to support children with social regulation challenges. It is important for therapists and teachers to understand how to effectively teach these skills; however, this work does not stop at school or in the therapy office. I know this both as a therapist who believes in a family-centered approach and as a family member of individuals with social challenges. In addition, I am a parent, and through research, as well as trial and error, I have practiced and refined many tips and tools to support my children's social and emotional growth. It happens seven days a week and needs to be infused into all aspects of the child's life and daily schedule. While this sounds like a tall order when added to everything else parents need to do on a daily basis, it can become part of the daily schedule without too much fuss or added stress, as illustrated in this book.

Therefore, including parents, other family members, and caregivers as social facilitators is essential for a child's success. This is the glue that makes the skills stick!

About This Book

This book is for parents, caregivers, teachers, and therapists who want to support children's social and emotional competence and participation. Specifically, children who have difficulty following directions, thinking about others, being flexible, reading nonverbal social cues, working in small groups, participating in conversation, advocating for themselves, seeing the "big picture," and making friends can benefit. However, the activities can enhance the social and emotional development of all children.

Make Social Learning Stick! offers a "social learning diet" that can be used in everyday life to increase verbal and nonverbal language, listening skills, understanding the hidden rules, perspective taking, executive functioning, and much more. Children need a steady intake of social examples, explanations, and practice throughout the day to help them understand these concepts. The activities presented in this book give an idea of what has worked for other families as well as help readers create their own ideas and "diet" of what might work for their unique child and family. In short, this book is not meant to tell parents to do extra work, but rather to utilize their natural routines to influence and increase social learning and to supplement teachings from outside professionals or other books that provide deeper and more specific social curriculum.

Many books provide the global view, or the whys of social and emotional development, and are designed for therapists. This book is more about the whats and how-tos – what to do in the moment and how to make the moment teachable. As a caregiver, you're probably already using a variety of strategies (consciously or unconsciously) to help your child develop better social skills and regulation. Take some credit and have confidence knowing that you're playing a vital role in making the child's social skills stick.

Make Social Learning Stick! also helps teachers and therapists provide practical suggestions for caregivers and equip them with the tools to practice and help generalize social skills into the natural setting from situation to situation. With over 185 fun and easy activities, including contributions from leading experts, this book shows how to take advantage of natural routines throughout the day and embrace teachable moments in order to increase social regulation.

Geared toward children preschool through elementary-school age, the ideas are meant to inspire creativity that suits the specific child's level and can be tailored to meet the child's skills or needs. Every child is different, and the suggestions are meant to be examples that can be customized and individualized for each child. If reading or writing is difficult, adapt the activity so that the child dictates to the parent or the parent reads to the child. If the child has sensory processing or physical challenges, modify the activity or suggestion and adjust it to the child's ability/capacity.

How the Book Is Organized

The book is divided into three major sections, (a) At Home, (b) In the Community, and (c) Holidays and Special Events, that focus on daily routines and give suggestions for increasing social participation within those routines and throughout the day. The book is not meant to be read from cover to cover, nor are the activities meant to be used in a particular order; however, the home section and some of the holidays are presented in chronological order to help with organization. Within each section, strategies are grouped by daily, weekly, and yearly activities and events that occur in most families' lives.

Each activity includes "hidden rules" – the unstated rules in the various social settings that we follow throughout our lives. For those who don't learn social norms intuitively, the hidden rules or "hidden curriculum" (Myles, Trautman, & Schelvan, 2013) can be confusing and need to be explained and reinforced on a regular basis. For example, we might think our children know that taking food off of another person's plate or taking up too much space on an airplane seat is considered rude, but they may not know these "rules." Review these social rules and remember to share them with the child either before, during, or after a social situation. As such, the book can be used as a starting point to discuss these various social situations and the social rules that go along with them.

Sprinkled throughout this book, you will find examples of an effective tool that Ward and Jacobsen (2012) call "job talk." These are tasks or actions (verbs) that are turned into nouns or "job talk" (see page 58 for more information). Simply adding "-er" to a verb or making the action into an occupation helps the child take ownership and become more willing to jump in and complete the task. For example, instead of saying to the child, "Can you help me sweep?," say, "Can you be the sweeper?" Or instead of saying, "Take a picture of that view," say, "You be the photographer." The examples are intended to serve as reminders to try out this tool to help the child initiate, take ownership, and increase motivation to do certain tasks. Job talk can be presented in the form of a question or a request. Give it a try; it's amazing how a small change in language can change a person's attitude!

Throughout the suggested activities you will also find user-friendly social learning vocabulary in italics. Many of the terms (but not all) are part of the Social Thinking Vocabulary developed by Michelle Garcia Winner. They provide a common language adults can use with children to describe the abstract concepts that are part and parcel of everyday social situations – concepts that we often have a hard time explaining. For example, we can say, *"keep your brain in the group"* when a child is daydreaming. This helps the child understand that she needs to be thinking about the subject at hand. It is more descriptive and, therefore, more concrete than saying, "stop daydreaming" or "pay attention." Refer to the back of the book for these vocabulary definitions and terms.

Finally, at the back of the book, you will also find tools and strategies to help you understand and implement the suggested activities, as well as a chart of all activities outlining the most pertinent area of social competence that they support.

Use, modify, or change the suggestions as you like, and realize that some activities may not work for your family. Use what you need, when you need it, and adapt the activities to fit. The hope is that these activities will spark new ideas that you can use and even share with others. Consider keeping this book in a place that is easily accessible to family members and caregivers so that they will remember to review and use the ideas throughout the day and be a part of the team that guides and supports the child's social and emotional development. The goal is to make social interactions fun and memorable while helping the child connect the dots. As you incorporate the activities into everyday life, the child will build comfort and skills in a broad range of social situations.

AT HOME

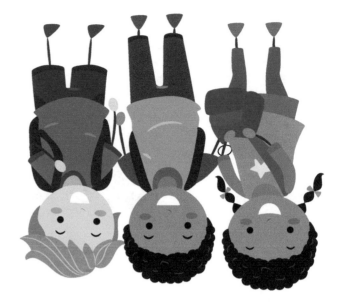

STARTING THE DAY

Mood Meter

Have the child check in each morning with a visual scale or meter (see page 72). Ask him to indicate how he is feeling. Encourage him to express his mood and explain why he is feeling that way. If he is feeling scared or upset about something, help him talk about why he is feeling that way and come up with a tool or way to make him feel better (e.g., taking a walk, thinking about something that makes him happy). Checking in like this throughout the day is a great way to regulate emotions and thereby prevent major behavioral outbursts.

Plan of the Day

Do some briefing/priming and talk about the "plan of the day" and what behavior is *expected* for each activity. Outline or map out situations that might be difficult, such as waiting in line at the grocery store or not being able to go to the park if it is raining. Don't forget to talk about the backup plan or Plan B in case something changes, such as going to the movies instead of the park if it rains. This practice will lessen anxiety and create more structure for children who need help with *flexible thinking*.

Job Talk: "You help be the planner."

Match the Picture

Take a picture of the child one day when he is dressed and ready to go to school with everything he needs to bring. The next day, help him get ready by showing him the picture and tell him that this is what it looks like when he is ready: hair brushed, fully dressed, backpack on, etc. Tell him to "match the picture." This is a tool for building a mental image of what he should look like in a given situation.

Contributed by Sarah Ward

Hidden Rules: 1. It may be *expected* to wake up groggy or grouchy, but it is *unexpected* to be rude or mean to others. 2. We all experience changes we cannot control, but it is *expected* that we control our reactions when we get frustrated or disappointed.

Rain or Shine?

When the child wakes up in the morning, have her look outside to determine the weather. Have her make a *smart guess* about the day ahead. Will they play outside for recess? Does she need an umbrella or jacket? Will soccer practice be cancelled? Life is filled with guessing, problem solving, and planning ahead.

Job Talk: "You be the weather reporter."

Planning Ahead

Mornings are often rushed and hectic, which can be frustrating for everybody. Have the child help you make lunches, get the backpack ready, and prepare an easy, healthy breakfast the night before. Make a visual schedule for the child's morning routine so that she knows what is *expected* and can *follow the plan*. Have her do as much as she can to get motivated and organized for the day. This is great for executive functioning and regulation.

Need a Pick-Me-Up?

If the child struggles to get out of bed in the morning and has a hard time getting ready for school or the day in general, practice various regulation tools, for example, taking a cold shower, exercising, or thinking about something she is looking forward to. Then put a photo of that activity on her nightstand to get her motivated to start the day.

GETTING READY FOR SCHOOL

What to Wear?

Have the child look outside to see what the weather is like. What clues does he see? Clouds? Sun? Rain? Have him help decide what to wear based on the clues he sees … if it's cloudy and cold, does he need a sweater? This is good for reinforcing the importance of observation and helps develop planning for the future and gaining foresight.

Hidden Rules: 1. What you might want to wear is not always appropriate; for example, PJs are meant to be worn at home, and Halloween costumes are for Halloween, not school days. 2. It is *expected* to wear warm clothes when the weather is cold and lighter clothes when it is hot. 3. Don't wear clothes that you can see through or that are too tight and show your underwear or privates. 4. If you don't get enough sleep and are drowsy at school, it is difficult to be social and focus in class, and it will make your teachers and friends have *unexpected* thoughts about you.

DINNER OR MEAL PREPARATION

Hidden Rules: 1. It's *expected* that people who are helping to make food wash their hands before helping out. 2. It's *expected* that you keep your hands and mouth out of the food when you are preparing it for others. 3. While cooking or handling food, pull your hair back or wear a hat. If the hair gets in the food, it is not only unsanitary, it will also make other people feel uncomfortable.

Where Did it Come From?

Ask the child to think about the origin of the food that is being served. When she realizes, for example, that farmers planted crops and harvested them, she can imagine what it might be like to work on a farm or that the various ingredients in the salad originated from many different places. If she needs help, provide a visual prompt from the box or bag label to show where the tomatoes came from. Once the child realizes all the hard work and thoughtfulness that goes into providing food and preparing meals, she might appreciate it more. This will help her realize that food doesn't just magically appear on the table.

Job Talk: "You can be the baker."

Making Dinner Together

Have the child help prepare dinner once a week. Activities like making a pizza can be a great sequencing lesson to build language. You can make index cards with photos (cut from magazines, coupons, or downloaded from the Internet) to show the steps needed to make the meal. For example, rolling out the pizza dough, spreading the sauce, sprinkling the cheese, baking the pizza, and then cutting it to eat. Sequencing is used for many skills in life, including executive functioning.

Food for Thought: What's for Dinner?

Encourage the child to look around and make a guess about what is for dinner ... what does he see? Smell? How is the table set? Have him ask questions to get clues. Once he has guessed what you are having for dinner, have him help determine what will be needed to go with the meal. If you are having bread, should we get the butter out? If salad, do we need dressing? This will help the child be a good social *detective* and make smart guesses.

Formal Dinners

Occasionally, have a "formal" dinner with just your family using cloth napkins, name cards, and formal place settings. You can have "formal" dinners once a month or more if you wish and have the time. The big pay-off is that when you have company for dinner or are invited out, your child will be familiar with the concept of "formal" dinner and be better able to handle differences like seating arrangements and cloth napkins.

Contributed by Kari Dunn Buron

Review the Rules

Sample Rules for Having FUN!

1. Keep your brain thinking about the other people playing (observing when it's their turn and watching how they are playing the game).
2. Keep your body connected with the people playing (face your friends and don't wander off).
3. Use a friendly voice, words, and actions.
4. Share your toys.

Have the child help you develop the rules and make a visual to refer to. This helps the child know what is *expected*, which helps him focus on the fun!

Play Nice and Add to the Fun

When interacting with others and the goal is to have fun, use the term "adding to the fun" as a friendly way to encourage positive behavior and attitude. Use the expression "taking away from the fun" to represent the opposite – an unfriendly way of playing. These terms can help kids understand how their behavior affects other people. We all like to have fun, so let's all do things to ADD TO THE FUN!

Fair Play

Teach the child how to use roshambo (also known as rock/paper/scissors) as a tool to resolve conflicts, such as which game to play, what rules to play by, or who should go first. This is a hand game where the players form one of three shapes with their hands to determine who is the winner. The "rock" beats "scissors", the "scissors" beats "paper" and the "paper" beats "rock." If players use the same shape, they are tied and have to do it again. This is a great way to settle disputes and compromise with others. It is similar to flipping a coin or drawing straws.
Contributed by Leah Kuypers

When All Else Fails, Vote!

Having members of a group vote or draw straws can be a good way to resolve a situation (e.g., what game to play). If they can't decide which game to play, narrow it down to 2-3 games and have them tally up who wants what or draw straws to pick the game of the day. This might be difficult if the vote is not in the child's favor, but it can be used as a teachable moment for learning about being flexible. This is an important skill, as voting will happen in many environments – at school, on the playground, etc.

Job Talk: "You be the voter."

PLAYING BY THE RULES

Following Someone Else's Plan

Make a list of the choices of games to play (e.g., *Checkers®, Connect 4®, Monopoly®*). Decide who will pick and lead the game. Determine a set time to play the game and follow the designated person's agenda. After that person's time is up, switch to follow another player's agenda and practice following her plan. This builds flexibility and compromising skills. This will help the child become a *flexible thinker.*

Job Talk: "Do you want to be the leader or the follower?"

Hidden Rules: 1. When you play by the rules, you add to the fun. When someone cheats, it takes away from the fun. 2. When you are bored or don't want to play a game any more, it's *expected* that you ask your friends if they are ready to play something else or finish out the game. You don't just walk away.

ENCOURAGING PLAY WITH PEERS AND SIBLINGS

Contributed by Pamela Wolfberg

Special Space

Create a special space for the child to play with other children.

1. Make the space safe, familiar, and inviting for all the children.
2. Include the child's favorite things that may be enjoyed with other children.
3. Organize the space with "play boxes" of favorite toys, activities, and themes.
4. Label the "play boxes" with visual symbols, such as a picture of a tent of a tent for camping theme.

Special Time

Devote special times for the child to play with other children.

1. Designate times for the child to play with peers on a consistent and frequent basis. For example, one hour after school on Tuesdays and Thursdays and two hours on weekends.
2. Create a visual schedule to help the child transition to this play routine. (See sample on page 77.)

Play Routines

Structure play sessions with consistent and pleasurable routines.

1. Opening routine: Start with a brief hello, guidelines for playing together, and an age-appropriate song or cheer. For example, have the children place their hands, one on top of the other, reach up, and call out, "Let's play!"
2. Guided play: Following the opening routine, set aside a longer period (30–45 minutes) for play.
3. Closing routine: End with cleanup, a snack, and good-bye song or cheer.

Have Fun!

Guide the children in mutually enjoyable play experiences, as follows.

1. Support children in finding common ground, building on the child's unique fascinations and favorite materials, activities, and themes. For example, if your child likes trains, ask the other children if they would like to play trains.
2. Follow the children's lead, allowing them to set the pace and flow of the experience. Start by connecting small trains and pushing them along a train track. Next, paint several small boxes as train cars and connect them with ropes so the children can pull each other around.

Hidden Rules: 1. Everyone loves to play with their favorite toy or focus on their area of interest. If you show interest in someone's interest, they will most likely do the same for you. 2. Siblings have feelings too, and although it can be a struggle to get along at times, you need to think about their feelings so they will think about yours, too.

Dress-Up

For young children, fill a box with dress-up clothes. Let the children put on the clothes and encourage them to pretend to be someone else or something else. Let the kid in you come out and model for them or follow the children's lead and become the patient if they are the doctor, for example. Pretending to be daddy, an animal, or some storybook character allows the child to step into someone else's shoes and builds perspective taking, which is an important interpersonal skill.

Pretend Play: Boxes, Boxes, and More Boxes

Kids love making houses, stores, castles, go carts, or rockets out of large cardboard boxes. Have them use these creations to invite friends to play with them or pretend with their stuffed animals. Practicing these imaginary skills at home with familiar people is excellent for building imagination skills and cognitive flexibility, which helps children to see things in different ways and from another person's point of view.

Write It Out, Act It Out

Have the child write a story (if she has trouble writing, you be the writer) and help the story come to life by acting it out with no voice. See if you can understand her nonverbal cues and what the story is about.

Job Talk: "Do you want to be the writer or actor."

Building a Fort

Put sheets over the top of a table, making it dark underneath. Put blankets on the floor with pillows, a digital clock, and flashlights. Pretend to have a party, picnic, or sleepover with the child's favorite stuffed animals, or invite a sibling, neighbor, or care-giver in for a visit. Have the child practice inviting, greeting, and how to be a good "host."   Prompt the child to extend her play to the next logical activity. For example, if you pretend to go camping, set up camp, and then prompt the child to pretend what might happen next (e.g., picnic or hike, followed by s'mores). This is great for thinking skills, specifically sequencing, planning, and developing forethought.

PRETEND PLAY

Role-Play

Make cards listing different social situations (e.g., going to a birthday party or inviting a friend to join your game) and role-play them with the child. This increases awareness of what these situations might look and feel like, including insight into other people's points of view.

Puppets: Using puppets to practice social situations is another way to act out what you'd like to see from the child and what to say or do to make others feel comfortable. Use the puppets to role-play and help the child problem solve. For example, develop and perform the show or help the child make a puppet show related to a social situation, having him use the puppets to act it out.

Stuffed Animals: Some kids find it easier to talk if they are doing it with a stuffed animal or puppet. Have available animals that represent different emotions and ask the child to use them to tell you about his day or emotional situation. As part of this activity (or once it's finished), refer to the mood meter (see page 72) and check in about how the child is feeling. If you don't have the mood meter nearby, ask the child to describe how the activity made him feel.

Hidden Rules: 1. When someone comes to your house to play, it is considered friendly to let her pick the game to play. 2. Part of playing a game is making sure it gets put away afterwards. If you put your games away, the pieces won't get lost, and you'll be able to continue to play with the game in the future.

INDOOR ANTI-BOREDOM

Hidden Rules: 1. Boring moments happen daily, and it's important to keep negative thoughts inside your brain by thinking about them as a "private thought" and not tell people that you are bored. 2. Nonverbal language is a much bigger part of communication than verbal language (research says more than 80%). Make sure to watch the face and body for these important messages. 3. When playing games, be careful to watch your personal space and don't get too close to others unless it's okay with them. Watching their facial expressions and body language will help you determine how close you can get.

Copycat

Have the child copy or imitate you engaged in social activities, such as talking on the phone, saying hello to a friend, asking social questions (e.g. "How was your weekend?" or "Did you enjoy the movie?"), making supportive comments (e.g. "Great job cleaning up the kitchen!"), making friendly facial expressions, etc. Imitation is one of the building blocks of social learning.

Job Talk: "You can be the server/waiter."

Cooking up Some Fun

Set up a lemonade or cookie stand and practice customer service with a smile. Rehearse with the child what to say ahead of time (e.g. "Hello, would you like some ice-cold lemonade?," "What else can I get for you?," "Thank you, come again."). This is helpful for building conversational skills and practicing making other people feel well taken care of.

Fun With Balloons

Help the child blow up balloons (one for each player or one for each hand if playing alone) and then let go of them. Make it into a race by seeing which balloon crosses a designated finish line or hits the wall first. Or blow up some balloons, tie them, and then play balloon toss back and forth, trying to keep the balloons up in the air as long as possible. Balloon volleyball is another fun game that can be played indoors with a partner. These types of games don't require much verbal language and can help build eye contact, cooperation, coordination, and flexibility.

Job Talk: "Do you want to be the dancer? I'll be the DJ/music player."

Freeze Dance

Get a group of people together. Assign one person to start and stop the music. When the music stops, everyone has to freeze. Anybody who moves is out. This is a great game to practice personal space and awareness of one's body in space and how we need to think about other people's boundaries. It is also good for regulating oneself in a group environment and being flexible (not taking it too seriously) when eliminated from the game. "Musical chairs" and "red light, green light" are other options for achieving these same goals. As part of this activity (or once it's finished), refer to the mood meter (see page 72) and check in about how the child is feeling. If you don't have the mood meter nearby, ask the child to describe how the activity made him feel.

Job Talk: "You can be a finder or seeker."

Scavenger Hunt

Place clues around the house and have the child hunt for them to find the final prize or answer. For example, "The first clue is on top of the large appliance that keeps food cold." When the child gets to the refrigerator, there is another clue, which might state something like, "The next clue is under the large pillow that you like to snuggle with" or "You can find the next clue by the jar with the sweet round treats." If the child doesn't read, use photos to direct her to the next clue or read the clues out loud. Being able to follow directions and look for clues is extremely important for social competence.

Job Talk: "You be a builder, hider, seeker, or player."

Nonverbal Games

Without using any words, try the following games/activities:

1. Build a tower with the child and take turns having one person be the builder and the others following the nonverbal directions (using only eyes, fingers, and body) for where the blocks should go.
2. Hide a toy and play "hot and cold" with no words. Have the child look for the toy and then look at your facial expressions to see if she is close to or far from the toy.
3. When playing a game, have all players use their eyes to determine whose turn it is by looking at the player. These games are helpful for increasing eye contact, understanding nonverbal clues, and thinking about others.

Place Setting

Have the child see what is for dinner. Then have her determine which utensils need to be placed at the table. Talk about who sits where and what each person might like to drink with the meal. This is great for practicing thinking about others.

Job Talk: "You be the place setter."

Vacuuming

Play a game about which piece of furniture or object needs to be moved next in order for you to be able to vacuum the floor or carpet. Move the vacuum cleaner near the piece of furniture and use gestures (e.g., smiles, thumbs up, or thumbs down) to show which one has to be moved. With the noise of the vacuum, it's crucial to understand gestures and facial expressions if you can't hear the words. This activity can help practicing being an astute observer and focusing on nonverbal cues. NOTE: This is not a good game for kids who are sensitive to loud noises.

Whose Clothes?

Ask the child to sort the laundry with you and have him make a *smart guess* about which clothes belong to which family member. Help him use the information that is available to him (e.g., size and style) to determine which clothes belong to whom. This encourages thinking about others and problem-solving skills.

Anything Can Be Turned Into Fun and Gains!

Tell the child that you are going to play a game. Similar to "I Spy," have the child be a detective and look for areas in the house that need cleaning or tidying up. Make a list of the things the child can do on his own, things you can do together, and things that need to be done by an adult. Have the child picture what it should look like when it's done; for example, can he picture what his bed looks like when it is made? Have him start with the things he can do on his own and praise him for helping around the house. Keeping the house clean is a family affair, and children can help support the family goals with a sense of pride.

Job Talk: "You be the house cleaner."

CHORES

Clear Vision for a Clean Future

Take photos of what you expect a room to look like when it's clean, or the toy or book area when straightened. Post it for the child to see, and when she is told to clean up, tell her to "match the picture." This helps build situational awareness and visualizing what a task should look like when completed.
Contributed by Sarah Ward

Job Talk: "You be the bed maker, room cleaner."

Hidden Rules: 1. It is *unexpected* to eat off a dirty plate. Make sure plates are clean before setting them on the table. 2. Plants need to be watered every few days; make a schedule and stick to it; don't wait for the leaves to turn brown. 3. If you have to vacuum, ask people if it's okay to turn on the vacuum so you are not disturbing somebody who might be sleeping, watching TV, or reading.

Hidden Rules: 1. Be careful about putting your hands near your pet's food when it is eating; it may bite you. 2. Always ask before petting someone else's dog.

FURRY FRIENDS

Emotional Benefits

Pets can help build emotional awareness and empathy and be great companions/friends. Have the child watch her pet and try to read its nonverbal cues to determine how it feels or what it wants (e.g., is it hungry? Tired?). If a dog looks sad because your child is leaving the house, talk about what might make it feel better (e.g., giving it a toy to play with while you are gone). Kids can count on their furry friends for some attention and companionship!

Job Talk: "You be the dog trainer."

Animals Help Cope With Emotions

Some people find that cuddling with a furry friend creates positive moods. When the child is feeling sad or upset, suggest that she curl up with her pet and take a break. She can even talk with her pet and tell it how she feels. Pets are great listeners and the most nonjudgmental members of the family! Pets can make the child feel less lonely and act as a supportive friend.

Job Talk: "You be the groomer, dog walker, brusher, and feeder."

Old Dog, New Tricks

Kids love to teach dogs tricks like sit, shake, and roll over. This can build expressive language and confidence when showing family members or friends what the child has taught the pet. As part of this activity (or once it's finished), refer to the mood meter (see page 72) and check in about how the child is feeling. If you don't have the mood meter nearby, ask the child to describe how the activity made him feel.

Caring for Pets = Building Responsibility

Pets need water and food to live. Create a schedule to feed and give water to your pet. This can be tied to a reinforcement system that you and the child develop together or be part of earning an allowance. Brainstorm what the pet needs in order to get exercise, stay clean, and feel loved. A bath? Brush? Walk? Caring for pets helps to build responsibility and confidence.

What's in a Name?

Have the child make observations about the family pet. What color is the fur? Does it have spots? Does it like to sleep a lot? Run around? After making these observations, pick a name that fits the pet. Brandy? Spot? Cuddles? This will help the child identify characteristics and make observations that can help with determining the best name for the pet.

Receiving a Call

Practice talking on the telephone with your child. Make sure that she listens for important information – who is calling, who the person is calling for, etc. If the child does not understand what is being said, help her ask for clarification (e.g., "I can't hear you, can you say that again?"). Use play phones to role-play to start, then practice on a real call with a familiar person. These are important life skills that all children need to learn.

Job Talk: "Be a receptionist."

Don't Be an Interruptosaurus!

Help the child notice when someone in your family is talking on the phone. What is the *expected* behavior? It is not a time to talk or ask for help except in an emergency. This is similar to interrupting people in a conversation. You can use the vocabulary "your words are bumping into my words" or "don't be an interruptosaurus" to help the child visualize how distracting interruptions can be.

Talking on the Phone

Establish guidelines for use of the telephone and discuss them with the family. Are you going to bring cell phones to the dinner table? Can you text during family time? By creating and following your own family guidelines, you prompt the child to think about the impact phone use has on other people in his social space and how it makes them feel. For example, explain that if you are on your cell phone, it can show that you are not thinking about the people around you, and it might make them feel less important.
Contributed by Kari Dunn Buron

PHONE ETIQUETTE

Hand Signals

Create hand signals to help the child predict the *expected* wait time when on the phone. For example, create a visual chart with an open palm indicating, "I can talk about this later," a hand with the index finger pointing upward indicating, "I can talk about this in a minute," and a hand shaped like a cup indicating, "I can talk now. I just finished my call."
Contributed by Emily Rubin

Hidden Rules: 1. When you answer the phone, say "hello," and before you hang up, say "good-bye." 2. Be careful about what time it is when you call people. Don't call early in the morning, during dinnertime, or late at night. 3. Never make prank phone calls; it is illegal, and you can get into serious trouble. 4. Keep your phone conversation short, and if the other person says he has to go, say good-bye and call back another time.

SHOWTIME

Job Talk: "You be the detective!"

Job Talk: "You be the observer!"

Reading the Visual Cues

With the child, pick a TV program or movie that includes characters who show clear and oversimplified emotions, facial expressions, and body language (e.g., *Wallace and Gromit, Charlie Brown*). Tell her that you will be pausing the show to talk about what's going on. After you have watched a bit together and the child has an idea of the characters and plot, pause and have her observe and talk about what the character might be thinking or feeling. Understanding nonverbal cues is essential for social interactions.

Teaching Social Skills Through Media

When watching movies, commercials, or films, comment on the actors' behaviors – how they are feeling, what's going on in the story, etc. Talk about their actions and how they make other people feel. If you see disrespectful or dangerous behavior, emphasize that such behavior is not OK in real life. For example, if a cartoon character is playing with a stick of dynamite, explain that this is dangerous and not a toy. TV programs and movies are filled with teachable moments and can help to develop an understanding of the emotions and thoughts of others and how behavior makes others feel.

Be a Family Detective

Present the child with three TV shows that she is familiar with and ask her which show she thinks each member of the family would want to watch and why. This is a great activity for learning to think about others and what they like.

Learning the Characters

During TV time, let the child choose a show. Ask her to identify one character in the show and explain who the character is and that his or her role is in the show. Help the child identify what this character likes or does not like and what her relationship is with the other characters on the show. This is great for learning perspective-taking.

Who Gets to Pick?

Create a family tradition of watching a TV show or movie together. Make a schedule of who gets to pick the show each time. Have the child make a *smart guess* as to what show he thinks each person will pick when it is their turn; this provides practice in being flexible if he doesn't want to watch a certain show.

I See What You're Thinking

While watching a TV show or movie, make up games to help the child learn about his own or others' perspectives and perceptions. Talk out loud about thoughts and feelings that come up. Start by getting the child to think about the thoughts and feelings that the characters/actors might be having, then have him identify his own thoughts and feelings about what he's watching. Lastly, see if he can "turn the tables" and determine how you or others watching the show might be feeling. Do you share the same thoughts and/or feelings, or are they different?

Contributed by Michelle Garcia Winner

A Picture Is Worth a Thousand Words

Pull out the family photo album and talk about activities that you did together and how you and everyone in the photo felt (e.g., choose a birthday party or a family vacation and talk about the fun that you had). This is a great activity to practice reading nonverbal social cues. As part of this activity (or once it's finished), refer to the mood meter (see page 72) and check in about how the child is feeling. If you don't have the mood meter nearby, ask the child to describe how the activity made him feel.

Emotions Scrapbooking

Look through magazines to find pictures with expressive faces. Cut them out and make a feeling collage. Label each photo with the emotion shown on the person's face. Talk about what makes you and the child feel the emotion depicted. Prompt if needed, such as model with your words what makes you happy or sad or give an indirect prompt by saying something like, "Didn't you feel sad the other day when you dropped your Lego structure and it broke?"

Family Tree

Make a family chart/tree using photos. Find a photo of each family member, tape or glue it onto a piece of cardboard, and under the photo write the name of the person and some things he or she likes. Conduct interviews with family members if needed to gain information. If appropriate, write a script of what to ask (e.g., "What are your favorite things to eat?," "What's your favorite color?"). This is a great way to practice thinking of others – perspective taking.

> *Job talk: "Do you want to be an interviewer or a reporter?"*

Thinking About the Family

Talk about things you like to do with each family member as well as what they like to do. Help the child draw a picture of herself and a family member doing an activity that they both enjoy. Model telling stories about family members and things you did with them. Help the child tell similar stories about family members and events. Sharing personal stories with friends and others is a great way to bond and build relationships, as well as gain a deeper understanding of who you are and where you come from.

Hidden Rules: 1. Some people enjoy talking about their family and childhood. Others find that hard to do. So if you ask somebody a question about his family and he changes the topic, move on to another topic. 2. People's favorite activities often change with age. What someone liked to do last year might be different this year; so ask to make sure.

FAMILY FIRST

I Think I'm Thinking!

Our goal with very young children is to help them become aware that they are having thoughts about things. Make it fun! When you and the child are together, do something very unexpected or silly. For instance, sit down on the floor while you're mixing cookie batter, or when it's time to watch a movie together, stand on the couch. Ask the child: "You're having a thought about me! What are you thinking?" Then reverse the idea. When the child is doing something wonderful, give her a big smile and a hug, and say, "I'm having a thought about you right now. I'm thinking you're so talented/terrific/generous," etc. Conversely, when the child is doing something she shouldn't, share your thoughts about the behavior: "I'm having a thought about you right now. I'm thinking you're supposed to be in bed and you're not. This makes me have uncomfortable thoughts about you."
Contributed by Michelle Garcia Winner

> *Job Talk: "You be the thinker."*

TALENT WANTED

Comic Relief

Jokes are a good way to teach the double meanings of words, "play on words," or puns such as "I went to a seafood disco last week … and pulled a mussel." Practicing jokes at the dinner table or during a family talent show can help prepare a child for telling jokes to friends. Jokes are a great icebreaker to make people feel comfortable, and humor is a great way to connect with others and build friendships. Warn the child that telling the same joke over and over to the same people ruins the fun. See page 78 for a list of kid-friendly jokes.

Talent Show

Hang a sheet or blanket in a doorway, grab a toy microphone or a hair brush, and put on a family talent show. This can include songs, skits, magic shows, reciting a poem or story, etc. Work towards putting on a show with multiple people. It's harder to coordinate group music bands or skits, and it helps practice working together as a group and thinking about others. This can build a child's confidence and help him participate in a school talent show with other children.

Charades

Make up cards with different emotions (e.g., happy, excited, mad, bored) and take turns acting out the feelings without using words or props. Other family members are to guess the emotion. After some practice, add actions (e.g., making a cake, riding a bike, having a birthday party). This is a great way to build nonverbal skills and interpreting others' nonverbal language.

Best in Show

Have the child teach your pet a trick and have them perform during a talent show or when people come over. Using pets and animals can be used as an icebreaker or point of interest to facilitate social interactions for many children.

Talent Comes in All Shapes and Sizes

Many children (and adults) don't like to perform in front of others, claiming that they don't have any talent. Try to think of things that the child can take pride in showing off, like knowing all the presidents, Pokémon® characters, or the train stations in your town. These are helpful and valuable skills and should be acknowledged.

Family Skits

Acting out a play or doing a skit is a great way to practice stepping into another person's shoes and thinking about what others might think about and how they act. Also, acting involves using and understanding nonverbal language. For example, if you have to perform in a play and pretend to be an animal, you have to think about what that animal looks and acts like and use those movements and gestures to act it out (e.g., an elephant walks slowly on all four legs with a trunk).

Hidden Rules: 1. Being on stage is fun, but time and space need to be shared so that others don't think you are hogging airtime and not sharing the stage. 2. Pets are good for showing off talent but make sure to treat them with respect and care. 3. Repeating the same joke over and over makes people annoyed and think you are not funny. 4. Be careful about telling jokes that make fun of other people or can be considered crude.

Job Talk: "You be the dog trainer, groomer."

Job Talk: "You are the actor, and we are the audience."

Job Talk: "You be a musician, poet, or a singer."

Handmade Thoughts

Help the child make friendship cards or draw a picture for a family member or a friend. Help the child think about the colors the person likes and write something nice that is specific to his relationship with the person. Does she have a pet that the child could draw or ask about? Has she been somewhere fun that the child could ask about? This kind of activity can help the child with conversation skills and connecting with others. As part of this activity (or once it's finished), refer to the mood meter (see page 72) and check in about how the child is feeling. If you don't have the mood meter nearby, ask the child to describe how the activity made him feel.

The Original Paper Doll

Draw pictures of faces with different mouths, eyebrows, eyes, and noses. Talk about the difference in the faces and the feelings/emotions that they show. Discuss how a smile vs. a frown or raised eyebrows vs. wrinkled eyebrows can change what message or expression the face shows. Model the expression yourself and encourage the child to do the same. This is great for learning to express and identify emotions.

Inside Others' Minds

Trace a family member's or friend's body on a sheet of butcher paper. In the space where the head or brain is, have the child draw things that she knows the person likes to think about. If she doesn't know what to draw, have her interview the person or ask questions to find out. This will help the child learn to think about the thoughts and desires of others – perspective taking.

Job Talk: "Do you want to be the drawer or writer?"

Drawing – Snapshot of a Child's Point of View

A drawing can help the child express himself, show what happened in a situation, or reveal his point of view. Use art as an opportunity or springboard for conversation or to help the child tell a story and talk or write about what is on his mind.

Job Talk: "You're the writer."

Visualizing With the End in Mind

Set out a yellow ("slow down and get ready"), a green ("do") and a red ("done") piece of construction paper. Print a picture of a craft you are going to do and cue the child that you start a task by thinking about what it will "look like" when you are done. Place the picture on the red paper and look at it to decide what you need to do to make the end product look like that. Write the steps or draw pictures of what you need to do on the green paper. Then look at the end picture and decide what materials you will need to gather to make the craft. Write those materials on the yellow paper. Don't just give the child the materials. Have her imagine the materials, think about where to find them and then collect the supplies. This teaches her to imagine her actions in her mind.

Contributed by Sarah Ward and Kristen Jacobsen

Pen Pals

Set up boxes around the house and help the child write letters and put them in the "mailboxes." If she needs help, write a template or have her draw pictures. Help the child think about things that she can share from her own life, including thoughtful comments and questions. Have her tell you when there is mail so you or a sibling can get the letters and write back. Refer to the mood meter (see page 72) to have the child tell you how she feels when she gets mail.

ARTS AND CRAFTS

Hidden Rules: 1. Don't draw on someone else's artwork unless you have permission. 2. Put crayons and markers back in the container when done using them so others can find them and so they don't make a mess or dry out.

IN THE KITCHEN

Social Contagion – The Domino Effect

Doing nice things for others can be contagious – have a domino effect. Have the child set up the dominoes, so to speak, by doing a kind gesture of clearing someone's plate or asking them if they want more to eat. Watch their facial expression, listen to their words, or watch for their action to see if the child's kind gesture draws them to do something nice for her such as washing the dishes.

To add to the contagion, have a cup or small jar for each family member, and when someone does something nice, put a rock or marble in the jar to represent that gesture. See how many marbles each person can get, talk about how they got the marbles, and praise them for caring about others. As part of this activity (or once it's finished), refer to the mood meter (see page 72) and check in about how the child is feeling. If you don't have the mood meter nearby, ask the child to describe how the activity made her feel.

1. Get Ready, 2. Do, 3. Done

Job Talk: "You be the waiter."

Start with a picture of what a food item looks like when prepared and ready to eat (e.g., what does a ham sandwich look like when done?). 1. Figure out what is needed to make it, and get all the ingredients (GET READY). 2. What will we need to do with the ingredients to put the sandwich together and make it "done"? (DO). 3. When you are finished, look at it to make sure it matches the picture or what you hoped it would look like (DONE). This activity is great for building executive functioning skills! See page 76. *Contributed by Sarah Ward and Kristen Jacobsen*

Service With a Smile

During TV or family time, have the child ask the people in the room if they would like anything to eat. See if the child can remember what they ordered and bring it to them like a waiter. This is great for improving memory and thinking of others.

Eyes Have Thoughts

Our eyes are powerful tools to help us understand the situation we are in. Following eye gaze can provide clues related to facial expressions, body language, and figuring out what someone is thinking about based on what that person is looking at.

The following strategy, called *thinking with your eyes*, is designed to suggest that we don't just look; we also think about what we're seeing. Practice this skill by making up games that don't include words in all sorts of settings. Start simple at first, just having the child follow eye gaze, and then add complexity as you go along. For example, when it's dinnertime:

1. Play "What am I looking at?" while you're making dinner. Ask the child to follow your eye gaze to look where you're looking and then figure out what you might be looking at. Make it obvious at first (look at the refrigerator or the frying pan in your hand) and then refine things as you go along (look at an egg or the spatula on the counter).
2. Take this idea to the next level and play "What am I thinking about?" Again, look at different things, but this time ask the child to guess what you're thinking about. For instance, if you're looking at the pitcher of ice tea, you might be thinking about the fact that you're thirsty. If you're looking at the clock, you might be thinking about the time dinner will be ready.

Contributed by Michelle Garcia Winner

Surprise Snack

Help the child make a snack for the rest of the family. First, brainstorm what they might like (e.g., popcorn if they are watching a movie, a popsicle if it is hot outside, or soup if somebody is sick). Then have the child serve the snacks and watch family members show appreciation with both their facial expressions and words. This builds positive reinforcement for thinking about others and taking their perspective. As part of this activity (or once it's finished), refer to the mood meter (see page 72) and check in about how he is feeling. If you don't have the mood meter nearby, ask the child to describe how the activity made him feel.

Hidden Rules: 1. Close the refrigerator door after opening it; leaving it open wastes energy and can make the food go bad. 2. Pour your milk, juice, or some other drink into a cup instead of taking the quick way and drinking it from the carton. 3. Wipe off the table or counter if you leave crumbs or a mess behind. 4. When the word "zapping" or "nuking" is used in the kitchen, it refers to cooking something in the microwave.

Talking Stick

Bring a microphone, spoon, or spatula to the table. Take turns passing it around, letting each family member use it as a microphone and "check in" about how their day went. Model giving one or two positives about the day and also something that was difficult or disappointing. For example, "I was happy when I finished a big project at work today, but it took extra time and I was frustrated that it delayed me in getting home on time." Use the mood meter (page 72) to help the child identify how she felt throughout the day.

Conversation Cards

Make and cut out conversation cards and place them in the middle of the table. During dinner, take turns picking up a card and asking and answering the questions. Use open-ended questions such as "What was the most fun part of your day?" or "What did you do in your after-school class today?" Practicing conversations at home helps with everyday conversation at school and beyond. See sample conversation cards (page 73).

Table Manners

Set up the expectations for what behaviors to demonstrate at the dinner table at home and in public (e.g., eating with your mouth closed, waiting until others are done eating before asking to be excused). Some rules are universal to all settings, such as eating with your mouth closed; others pertain more to eating in public places, depending on how strict the rules are at your home. Either way, the child should be aware of what might be *expected* or *unexpected* when eating with others. Have the child watch and learn from others. Make a game out of it, whereby the child observes others and notices when other people at the table are following or not following the family table manners.

Job Talk: "I will be the talker, and you can be the listener."

AT THE TABLE

Wonder Questions

Make a written visual cue or prompt of the type of questions that may be asked during dinnertime. Wh-questions (*who, what, which,* etc.) are great for wondering about others. When the child is able to ask questions using the visual prompt, take it away and only present it if she seems to struggle to remember how to start a sentence. See the wonder questions (page 74) for examples.

Dinner Schedule

Make a visual schedule showing the expectations for dinnertime. This will help set your family up for success and know what is *expected*. See the dinnertime schedule (page 75) for an example.

"Eye See You"

Often we can determine what someone is thinking about just by observing and determining what he is looking at (refer back to Michelle Garcia Winner's contribution on page 24). Practice this skill by making up games that don't include words; for example,

1. When it's time to sit down and eat, have one person be the seat assigner and have him use his eye gaze to show where everyone is supposed to sit.
2. When someone wants something passed to her at the table, have her make her needs and wants known by using gestures and eye contact only.
3. Offer choices of food or drink (e.g., water or milk) and have the person indicate what she would like by looking at the desired item – no words allowed.

Hidden Rules: 1. Don't "yuck" another person's "yum." Sometimes what you dislike is delicious to others. Don't make negative comments about someone else's food. 2. Ask before taking or eating off someone else's plate. 3. It is considered rude to reach over the table to get something. Instead, ask someone, "Pass it, please." 4. Be sure to keep your mouth closed while you are chewing food and wait to talk until you have swallowed your food. 5. Wash your hands before eating a meal.

Show and Tell

Have family members take turns showing something special and telling about it at the dinner table. This can be anything from a drawing, a special coin, or a book you are reading. This activity is great for practicing taking turns and conversation.

NIGHTTIME ROUTINE

How Was Your Day?

Start the bedtime routine early so you have time to talk with the child about how her day went. You will be amazed at how much more children share at this time of day – most children will do anything to stay up, even share the activities of their day! Encourage the child to ask about your day. Make sure to offer something you found upsetting and how you handled it, along with the good stuff. For example, say, "I got stuck in really bad traffic and that made me late to pick you up from school. This stressed me out, but I really enjoyed reading with you tonight; that was fun." Use the mood meter (see page 72) if the child needs help identifying how she feels and how the facial expression might look when she feels that way.

Observing Acts of Kindness

Ask the child to tell you something he saw during the day that showed someone doing something helpful or saying something nice to someone. This brings awareness and gives ideas for how to show acts of kindness.

Nighttime Routine

When asking the child about her day, it is helpful to use a rating scale so she can label the emotion she felt about the various things that happened. You can use something like the following or make up your own scale, using your own words:

5 = This made me feel awesome!
4 = This made me feel very happy!
3 = This made me feel comfortable/OK.
2 = This made me irritated.
1 = This made me feel angry or mad.

(See sample 5-point scale for nighttime routine on page 79.)

Contributed by Kari Dunn Buron

Calming Strategies – Winding Down

Before bed is a perfect time to talk with children about tools they use to calm their bodies and emotions. Practice taking deep breaths when in a calm state so it will be easier to use when escalated. Teach deep breathing by:

- Having the child imagine he's blowing up a balloon in his tummy and then slowly releasing the air.
- Placing an object on the child's stomach and having him watch it rise up and down with his breath.
- Pairing language with the breathing, such as "smell the flowers" (breathe in), "blow out the candles" (breathe out), etc.

Contributed by Leah Kuypers

Gratitude

Before bed, have the child recall one friend, family member, or person that she saw that day that she is thankful for and tell why. Provide a model or indirect verbal prompt by saying something like, "It was great to watch you play with your cousin today. I saw him share his toy with you. That must have made you feel thankful and happy." Help her see how relationships and people can add to her life and that we should be grateful for that. Modify the "I Am Thankful For" visual on page 81 if you want a visual prompt for this activity.

Sweet Dreams

Before the child falls asleep, encourage him to think about things that make him happy and people he might want to dream about. Tell him to try to remember his dreams so he can share them in the morning and practice telling stories about the fun he had while he slept. This is another good topic for conversation.

Hidden Rule: 1. It's *unexpected* to use or touch someone else's toothbrush; it can spread germs. 2. Always wash your hands after using the bathroom. 3. Avoid discussing your bathroom activities or asking others about theirs; it is considered private. 4. Bedtime is a time for winding down and being quiet.

Scrubbing Is Loving

Help the child understand that good hygiene is important, not only for keeping clean and preventing the spread of germs but also for conveying a message or impression to other people of how we value ourselves. Teach the child to wash his face, body and hair and brush his teeth. Tell him the importance of this during the early years so when he is a teenager this will already be a routine and easy for him.

Job Talk: "Be a good tooth brusher, face washer, etc."

Follow the Steps

If the child has difficulty following all the sequences of bathing, brushing her teeth, washing hands, etc., make a visual checklist or chart to aid with proper hygiene. See visual for brushing teeth on page 82. This will help with independence and completing these tasks in a timely manner.

Job Talk: "Can you be a bather, scrubber?"

Mirror, Mirror

Write down or cut out pictures of a variety of emotions and place them in a jar in the bathroom. While completing grooming activities, draw a slip of paper with an emotion and use the mirror to explore the facial expression and body language that correspond with it. This can turn into a guessing game, so the child is not only working on increasing her ability to display a variety of emotional expressions but also on improving her ability to read others' emotions and body language.
Contributed by Leah Kuypers

Make a Splash

If the child enjoys taking a bath, use this time as a teachable moment to practice sharing imaginary thoughts. So many things during bath time can be used for imaginary play, such as making the bubbles into a mountain of snow or turning the washcloth into a boat that sinks in the water. You can also use toys, sing songs, or play hide-and-seek with the washcloth to engage and have fun while getting clean.

IN THE BATHROOM

Hidden Rules: 1. Close the door when you're using the bathroom. 2. Always knock and wait to see if someone answers before opening a closed bathroom door. 3. Flush the toilet and wash your hands after using the bathroom, and don't talk about what you did in the bathroom. 4. Pull up your pants and zippers or get your clothes situated before you leave the bathroom.

STORY TIME

Job Talk: "Be the storyteller."

Job Talk: "Be a good listener."

Job Talk: "You be the predictor."

Job Talk: "You be the guesser."

Stepping Into the Character's Shoes

It is difficult for many children to understand the perspective of characters in a story. Yet, this is a very important skill to master for reading comprehension. Begin by choosing simple books with one main character. After reading the book, talk about the character and what the child learned about him or her. Make guesses about what the character likes and doesn't like; how he/she feels, and how the other characters in the book perceive him/her. Take your time; this can be more difficult than you think. For example, if the child is reading *Harry Potter*, have her think about what Harry likes (e.g., Quidditch and owls).

Listening With the Whole Body

Reading time is a great opportunity to practice listening with the whole body. Have the child use his eyes to look at the book and his ears to hear the words, keep his hands, feet, and body still, mouth quiet, his brain to think about the story and heart to care about what he is hearing and the person reading to him. When he uses whole body listening, it is easier to stay focused and enjoy the book. See visual on page 84 to remind the child of how to use whole body listening.

Reading/Literacy

Find books about children or characters who have social problems or differences that make their lives difficult in some way. Talking about fictional characters with social problems is far less personal than talking about our own problems. You and the child can come up with creative and fun ideas for how the fictional character can solve his problem. This practice can make it easier for him to eventually solve some problems of his own.

Contributed by Kari Dunn Buron

Hidden Rules: 1. When someone is reading to you, it is *expected* that you pay attention and focus on the story. 2. Be careful with books so that they don't rip when you turn the page.

Wordless Picture Books

Find picture books without writing (wordless books). Have the child look at the pictures and try to figure out what's going on. What are the clues? Have her tell the story to you. Occasionally, pick a picture from the book and ask the child what she thinks will happen to the character immediately, within the next 10 minutes, after an hour, and tomorrow. This is great for increasing expressive language and critical thinking. Retelling stories also helps to increase conversational skills.

Contributed by Sarah Ward

Story Telling

Cut out pictures from magazines or use family photos from a specific event and place them in a box. Take turns pulling out the photos with the child and practice telling what happened. For example, "The two boys are at the zoo and looking at the animals." or "This is on the beach in Hawaii when we were there on vacation two years ago; we made a sandcastle." The visuals serve as a prompt to help the child recall and tell stories, which is what we naturally do in conversation when we are sharing experiences with someone.

Finishing the Story

Use the same photos and activity as above, but stop the story so that the child can add to it, continue it, or change it to make it longer or different, such as adding another day to the vacation. You can use a direct verbal prompt if needed. "This is a photo of when we went to Hawaii, remember that? Tell me what else you remember doing there and what you would do if we could have added another day to the trip." Being a good storyteller is important for conversations and reporting on experiences and observations.

Guessing What the Book Is About

Take out a book the child doesn't know and have her look at the cover image. Have her guess what the book is about. While reading the book, have her guess what's going to happen next. Looking for clues and making inferences about what will happen helps the child in school and social situations.

IN THE COMMUNITY

IN THE CAR

Hidden Rules: 1. When you're in the car, it is *expected* that you stay seated, keep your seat belt on, and keep your hands and feet to yourself. Do not distract the person who is driving. 2. When getting out of the car, it is safer to get out on the side close to the sidewalk. If you get out on the side with traffic, use caution when opening the door and getting out. 3. When getting out of the car, keep your feet on the floor and don't step on the seats of the car. 4. Keep your feet on the floor when you are sitting, and not on the seat in front of you.

"I Spy ..."

Play "I Spy" and try to make *smart guesses* about what you or the child is seeing outside the car window and, therefore, might be thinking about (e.g., "I spy an animal on a leash." ..."Yes, it's a dog. What do you think I'm thinking about if I'm looking at the dog?"). Being able to determine what someone is looking at can be the first step to figuring out what they are thinking about. Being able to understand what other people are thinking about is a major part of what we mean by perspective taking.

Set the Child up for Success – "Priming"

On the way, discuss where you are going and what is *expected* of the child when you get there. Will he have to be quiet and polite or can he play and run around? If this is the first time at a given destination, explain who will be there and what will be happening. Should the child be focusing on one person (e.g., the birthday boy)? If you're visiting somebody's home, help the child think of things that person likes to talk about (e.g., what are her top three favorite things to do?). This kind of priming increases his level of confidence and helps him think about the person you are visiting and understand how to act. In addition, it lessens his anxiety and thereby the chance of meltdowns. Finally, it also increases his mental picture and situational awareness for the future (forethought).

Debriefing

On the way home, use the car ride to do some debriefing or perform a "social autopsy" (see page 87) by reviewing and reflecting on what happened. Use these teachable moments to talk about what went well and what the child could do differently next time. For example, ask, "How do you think the birthday went? How do you think Sam felt when you gave him his birthday present? How do you think he felt when you put your finger in his cake without asking?" We can all learn from our mistakes and increase the ability to use hindsight. As part of this activity (or once it's finished), refer to the mood meter (see page 72) and check in about how the child is feeling. If you don't have the mood meter nearby, ask him to describe how the activity made him feel.

Same But Different

If you are going to a new place but one that is similar to places you have visited in the past (e.g., a new movie theater), use priming and help the child identify how the new place will be the same but different (e.g., the concession stand is smaller, the seats are different). This will help her create a mental image of what to expect and be flexible about the fact that it isn't the same as the movie theater that she usually goes to. As a result, this may prevent possible behavioral outbursts caused by anxiety.

Job Talk: "You be a comparer."

Would You Rather?

While on the go (e.g., running errands, between school and appointments), use the time to play games, such as asking questions like "Would you rather eat mushrooms or spinach?," "Would you rather go camping or skiing?," "Would you rather watch a baseball game or go to the movies?" Have the child answer why or why not, and then have her ask you similar questions. This is great for building curiosity and learning about other people. See sample "Would You Rather" questions on page 85.

Guess the Destination

Help the child make inferences by paying attention to people in the street. Do they have a suit on? Gym clothes? Are they the mail carrier? Help the child read these social cues and make a smart guess about their vocation and where they might be going. Games like this are good for learning real-life predicting skills.

Job Talk: "You be the question asker, and I'll be the question answerer."

Share Your Feelings

If there is a lot of traffic or you are running late, express your feelings of stress and tell the child how you are working on staying calm by using a tool that helps you (e.g., listening to classical music, using self talk). Ask the child what he would do to keep himself calm and if he has any suggestions for you. It's important for children's social emotional growth to see that we all work on keeping ourselves calm in stressful situations.

"B.I.N.G.O. Was His Name – O"

Create a social Bingo game for the car. Find photos of people of a variety of ages and paste them on a sheet of paper. While you're in the car, have the child make guesses about places you pass where these people might like to go. For example, if you have a photo of a boy and you pass a toy store, see if the child can tell you why the boy would want to stop there.

Time to Listen

Turn off the radio and tune into the child. Ask open-ended questions such as "Can you tell me about the best part of your day?" to get her to share information about her social life and practice conversational skills. Talking in the car is often beneficial for a child who feels pressure, overwhelmed, or uncomfortable with direct eye contact or body language.

Job Talk: "Do you want to be the talker or the listener?"

IN THE CAR

Hidden Rules: 1. Traffic can cause stress. When there is a lot of traffic, be sure to be quiet so the driver can focus on the road. 2. People don't like to have a dirty car, and it is *expected* that you take your trash with you when you get out. Don't throw it out the window. 3. It is *unexpected* to yell or make negative faces at people outside the car.

Why Are We Here?

Tell the child that you're going to the mall and that you're going to play a game where she will be a social *detective*. It's the child's job to try to figure out why you're going there or what you need to buy. Help her ask Wonder Questions (see page 74) (e.g., "What size is it? Who is it for?") to determine the reason for going shopping. Observing social situations and making *smart guesses* about the information you know and observe is an important part of social competence. This game keeps the child engaged, focused on the activity, and teaches her to problem solve and follow the plan – skills all good shoppers can benefit from.

Job Talk: *"Do you want to be the researcher or detective?"*

Asking for Help

Pretend you don't know where to find something in the store and ask the child to get help from the store clerk. Make sure that he gets the clerk's attention in an *expected* way (e.g., "Excuse me, can I ask you a question?") and that he is able to retain the information to give back to you. Knowing how to ask for help and advocate for oneself is a valuable life skill that needs to be taught to all kids, but especially those with social challenges.

Job Talk: *"Can you be a people watcher?"*

"Do You See What I See?"

Find a place to sit and relax at the mall and ask the child to observe the people who walk by or are sitting near you. Does he see someone who looks like she's going into a pet store? Does she have a furry friend at home? Compare your social observations to see if they are similar to the child's, and then talk about the importance of making guesses. When we're engaging with other people, we need to make observations and think about what they might be thinking about and, therefore, what they might want to talk about.

AT THE MALL

What's My Perspective?

Start by creating some simple thought and emotion cards using index cards and a marker. Write down one word or phrase on each card. Thinking cards might include: That was nice! That was silly! I like that! I hate that! That's good! That's not so good. Emotion cards might include happy, sad, scared, mad, OK, frustrated, etc. Match the thinking and emotion words to the child's social level. Use the cards when you're together in different situations to explore your thoughts and feelings – same or different perspectives. For instance, while you're at the mall, sit together and people watch. Pick out someone wearing odd clothes, or a group of guys who are acting goofy. Have the child pick a thought or emotion card that reflects her perspective. Then you do the same. Talk about whether your perspectives were the same or different.

Contributed by Michelle Garcia Winner

Coping With Emotions

Use social briefing to help the child predict *expected* ways to cope with emotions that may arise at the mall (e.g., excitement, disappointment, hunger). For example, if it is close to dinnertime and you know the child will want a cookie when she smells the cookies being made at the cookie store, tell her that she can't have a cookie this time because it is too close to dinner. With the child, create a set of cue cards before the trip to the mall or elsewhere that may be attached to your purse on a key ring to display an emotion (e.g., disappointment) on one side and *expected* coping strategies on the reverse (e.g., we can take a photo or write down an item we cannot buy today and then add it to your wish list). *Contributed by Emily Rubin*

Job Talk: *"You be a door holder!"*

"Hold the Door, Please"

Have the child practice holding open the door for people when they walk in or out of a store. Encourage him to watch people's faces and see if he can tell how his kind gesture of holding the door made them feel.

Hidden Rules: 1. It is *unexpected* to touch merchandise that you don't intend to buy. 2. Most stores don't allow you to bring food or drinks inside. 3. Calculate the change/money that you expect to get back before buying an item so you don't take too much time at the register when it's your turn. 4. Always wear socks when trying on shoes (most shoes stores have throw-away socks you can use if necessary) and underwear when trying on clothes (especially when trying on a bathing suit) in a store.

Sharing Is Caring

Bring a toy and help the child share it with a new friend. Help her initiate and invite a child to play. Then have her practice being flexible and letting others use her toy or letting them go first at a game.

Job Talk: "Be the inviter."

Choosing Friends

Practice observing other kids at the park with the child. Help him observe and find a child who might have the same interest as his (e.g., more physical, playing with trucks, digging in the dirt). This activity will build his observation skills and lessen the chance of rejection by kids he approaches.

Social Exposure

Even if the child is not ready to play in larger groups or with other kids on the playground, encourage her to spend time at the park, play with an adult or sibling, and be in close proximity to other children playing. Help her observe other children and notice what they are doing. Through this experience, she can also get used to the sounds, sights, and smells found in most parks and outdoor areas.

AT THE PLAYGROUND OR THE PARK

Snow or Sand Trails

See if you can find other people's footprints in the snow or sand. With your child, follow the footprints and help him imagine where the trail ends, where the person might have been going, or what he might have been doing. Help him step into someone else's shoes by literally "walking in someone's footsteps."

Sharing Your Imagination

If there are clouds in the sky, lie down on the ground with the child. Looking at the sky, ask him to imagine that the clouds are animals or objects. *Share your imagination* with each other and compare what you see. Always encourage creativity and even "outlandish" imagination; the child may be the next great inventor.

Partner and Group Activities

Tag, chase, and ball toss can be great fun for kids and build reciprocal play and interaction. When it's hot, fill water/squirt bottles with water to use in a game of tag. Use balloons for dodge ball or to toss back and forth. Another favorite is ice races where children balance a piece of ice on a spoon and race across the yard. This can be done with one other person or in teams/group of kids. Take it slow with group games; they require a lot of social smarts and flexibility. Also, the child might be sensitive to loud sounds or the way the water/ice feels on her skin. Sensory issues are important to consider when playing with others.

Hidden Rules: 1. It is *unexpected* to take other kids' toys at the park without asking. 2. Don't throw anything (e.g., sand or rocks) at others. The exception is a ball if you are playing ball. 3. If you find toys at the park that are not yours, it is best to leave them in case someone comes back to look for them.

Job Talk: "Do you want to be the tagger? Chaser? Tosser? Thrower? Runner?"

AT THE GROCERY STORE

Hidden Rules: 1. It is *expected* that you walk in the grocery store and be careful not to block other people with your cart. 2. It is *expected* to smile and be friendly to the people around you. 3. Wait to eat food until you have paid for it; you will get in trouble for tasting or eating food before it's purchased, unless there is a special tasting display. 4. Keep to yourself negative comments about the food that others are buying; it's *unexpected* to say things to strangers such as "That food is bad for you."

Food Routes – Connect the Dots!

When you are in the produce section of the grocery store, check the labels on the fruits and vegetables to see if you can determine where a particular item was grown. Talk about the different climates in those states or countries and discuss how the particular food got to the store. This encourages perspective taking as the child realizes that food comes from different places and that it can often be a complex process to get it to the store.

Job Talk: "You're a great smiler/greeter/door holder!"

Helping Hands

Model kindhearted gestures such as holding the door open for someone, asking if somebody needs help carrying their groceries, or greeting the store clerk with a smile. Encourage the child to help unload the groceries with you, and provide verbal praise for his efforts, telling him how helpful it is. Let him know that it is nice to be helpful and kind to others.

Job Talk: "Can you be the shopper?"

What Aisle?

Make the child responsible for part of the grocery list. See if he can determine where items are located in the store based on the categories in each aisle and section. Provide prompting if needed, such as the indirect prompt, "If all the salad stuff is in the produce section over here, where do you think we can find the lettuce?"

Job Talk: "You be the list maker."

Grocery List

Have the child help make up the family grocery list. Model how to go through the cupboard and refrigerator and ask her to guess what you need to buy at the store. To eliminate a list of candy and soda, use a typed list of standard items and have her check off what is needed. This will help the child develop planning and organizational skills. See sample grocery list on page 86.

Step by Step

On the way to the restaurant, see if the child can sequence all the steps that are involved in eating dinner at a sit-down restaurant:

1. Pick the restaurant.
2. Get there.
3. Greet the host.
4. Wait for a table.
5. Sit down.
6. Order your food.
7. Wait for the food.
8. Eat.
9. Pay the bill.
10. Leave the restaurant, etc.

If the child is a picky eater, help her plan ahead for what she might order and let her know she might need to be flexible if they don't have what she wants. She might have to order spaghetti instead of macaroni and cheese.

What Are You Going to Have?

Look at the menu and ask the child to make a *smart guess* about what the people at your table or in your family will order based on what she knows they like to eat. Model this by saying, "The last two times we were here, dad got the chef salad. I bet he'll have that again because he was saying how much he likes it."

Social Spying

Help the child observe others and try to determine what their relationship is to each other (e.g., mom and son, husband and wife, grandma and granddaughter). Reading these types of social cues helps the child increase her *social detective* skills.

Job Talk: "Be a social detective!"

Chef for the Day

Help the child imagine what it would be like to be a chef and think about all the things that he would have to do to run a kitchen and make the food just the way that everyone likes it. This is a great way to "step into someone's shoes" and take perspective.

Job Talk: "Can you pretend you're the chef?"

EATING OUT

Hidden Rules: 1. It is *expected* that you are patient and wait while food is prepared and delivered to your table. Don't ask the waiter when your food will be ready. 2. When you're finished eating your meal, wait for others to finish before getting up to leave. 3. Take part in the conversation at the table. 4. It's *expected* that you stay off your phone and pay attention to the other people at the table when eating with others.

AT THE DOCTOR'S OFFICE

Hidden Rules: 1. While waiting for the doctor in the examining room, it is important to be quiet and not touch the equipment that is on the counter or in the drawers. 2. It is *unexpected* to ask people in the waiting room why they are at the doctor's office or to tell them why you are there.

Validating Feelings

If you suspect the child is nervous about going to the doctor, let her know that this is a typical feeling on such occasions, and provide her with some calming tools that you know work for her (bring a favorite toy, book; do some deep breathing, etc.). Tell her how you keep yourself calm when you go to the doctor.

Do a Practice Run

Role-play and act out what it's like to go to the doctor. Practice sitting in a waiting room quietly and getting an exam. Reverse roles, and have the child give you an exam to show that you have to visit the doctor some-times, too. Write a brief story or check out a book about going to the doctor for the child to read and review to prepare him for what to expect. Show him photos of waiting rooms and doctors' offices to give him a visual of what it will look like. This will help reduce anxiety about the unknown.

Analyzing Ads

While in the waiting room, look at magazines and have the child guess what products or services the advertisements are marketing without looking at the words.

Guessing Your Stats

Have the child make a *smart guess* about how much he weighs and how tall he is based on what his stats were the last time he was at the doctor's.

Preshow

While waiting for the movie to start, talk about what you already know about the movie and predict what you think it will be about. This builds perspective taking and the ability to think ahead (forethought).

Quiet in the Theater

Review all of the steps for whole body listening (see page 84) and discuss the importance of this type of listening in the movie theater (i.e., even though you're not talking to someone directly, you're sharing space with others who are trying to listen to and watch the movie, too).

Job Talk: "Be a good listener."

Post-Show

When the movie is over, talk about what you liked and didn't like about it. Try to recall the events and help the child come up with 3-4 main points that she can share with another family member or friend without giving away the whole plot. Rehearse before sharing to build confidence.

Job Talk: "You be a movie critic."

The Spotlight's on You

Ask the child to pick a character from the movie and have him describe what he knows about that person. Have him step into the character's shoes and try to feel what it would be like to live his/her life. This is great for building perspective taking and empathy.

AT THE MOVIES

Hidden Rules: 1. It is *expected* that you are quiet and keep your feet and hands to yourself in the movie theater. 2. Unless they ask you, it is *unexpected* to tell others how the movie ends if they haven't seen it yet. 3. It is OK to eat and drink at the movies but do it quietly so it doesn't bother others. 4. Most theaters don't let you bring your own food.

AROUND THE NEIGHBORHOOD

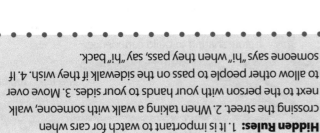

Hidden Rules: 1. It is important to watch for cars when crossing the street. 2. When taking a walk with someone, walk next to the person with your hands to your sides. 3. Move over to allow other people to pass on the sidewalk if they wish. 4. If someone says "hi" when they pass, say "hi" back.

Exploring Your World

Have the child make a list of the things that she sees on the way to school, the park, or around your neighborhood. Have her explore, observe, and gather information to share with the family. Did she notice that someone got a new mailbox or is preparing to paint their house? Did she see new flowers coming up, or someone planting new bushes? Observing and sharing thoughts is an important part of relating to others.

Job Talk: "Be an explorer!"

Pay It Forward

Help the child start a kindness campaign and have her "pay it forward" by doing nice things or volunteering for people in the neighborhood (e.g., bringing them their garbage, making them food, taking out their garbage, offering to walk their dog). Give them a postcard that says to pay it forward with someone else. This is a wonderful gesture and great way to think about other people's needs.

Who Are the People in the Neighborhood?

On your walks, help the child make observations about the environment. If he sees a house where there are toys on the front porch, does he think children live there? If he sees a cat on the prowl, does he think a bird might be nearby? If there is a doghouse in the yard, does he think the neighbors have a dog? Putting the social pieces together helps to understand the entire puzzle.

Safety First – Don't Talk to Strangers

Talk to the child about who to talk to and who not to talk to. Friendly greetings are *expected* when you already know someone. However, when you don't know someone, it is *unexpected* to talk to them. Going for a walk in the neighborhood is a good time to practice friendly behavior vs. community awareness and safety.

Friendly Greetings

Walk in your neighborhood and have the child practice greeting your neighbors with a warm smile, a friendly head nod, or a verbal "hello." Maybe even have her ask how a neighbor's day was or how her dog is doing. A final "nice to see you" is a great way to end greetings. If the child is not comfortable with this, model these behaviors while she observes.

Job Talk: "You be a greeter!"

Playing Ball

Playing sports offers lots of teachable moments. If the child has the skills and desire, have her participate in group sports and talk with her about the rules and what is *expected*. Practice what she will say if her team wins vs. loses and how the others might feel if she says something unsupportive. Being a "good sport" and practicing sportsmanship can take lots of practice, but it's important for building teamwork and flexibility. In addition, it's great exercise.

Watching Sports

Taking the child to a sports event can be fun but may also be challenging because of the logistics, including crowds and emotions invested in wanting your team to win. Turn such events into teachable moments. For example, even if someone is cheering for the other team, make supportive comments. Don't talk "trash" (i.e., poorly) about other people's viewpoints. Be a good role model and practice at home while watching sporting events on TV. Start by going to smaller sports venues with familiar people before attempting a large crowd with strangers.

Job Talk: "Can you be a spectator and a cheerleader?"

Building Emotional Vocabulary Can Be a Sport in Itself!

Sporting events and intense emotions go hand in hand. Help the child build his emotional vocabulary and awareness by pointing out the various emotions players and fans are experiencing. Such emotions may include disappointed, upset, worried, motivated, competitive, elated, frustrated, confused, furious, ecstatic, exhausted, and many more. You can also discuss whether a given emotion was *expected* or *unexpected* given the circumstances. For example, if your team scores and the fans are cheering, that is *expected*, but if a fan from the opposite team yells bad words, that is taking it too far and is considered *unexpected*.
Contributed by Leah Kuypers

SPORTS EVENTS

Hidden Rules: 1. When playing a game with someone, it is *expected* that you finish the game, even if you are losing. 2. Everyone wants to see the action; don't block other people's view. 3. If someone gets hurt in a sports game, show support by clapping when they get up or are assisted off the field.

TRANSITIONS

Hidden Rules: 1. Watch out for the size (i.e., intensity) of your reaction. If you have big reactions (e.g., yelling and crying) to something small like your shoe being untied, others might feel uncomfortable and not want to be around you. 2. Use a quiet voice in the library, and if you need help finding something, go to the information table and ask in a low voice. 3. Even when things are planned out, sometimes they change and you have to follow an alternative plan. Try to stay flexible and positive and positive.

Life Happens

Talk with the child about being flexible when things don't go the way that he planned. Be a good model and talk with him about taking a different route to get somewhere or different ways of doing things. This will show him that sometimes we have to come up with a Plan B and change our plan or action or thoughts to stay calm and achieve our goals.

Hidden Rules Change From Situation to Situation

Take the child to various locations (the library, grocery store, etc.) and have her observe and possibly write down notes in a notebook about how people interact differently in each situation or environment. Once she gets the idea that the rules for how to behave change depending on the setting, have her predict what the rules might be. For example, after realizing that people talk quietly in the library, have her tell you the hidden rules of the library before entering. When you are headed to a new location, have her make a *smart guess* or come up with a hypothesis for what she thinks might be *expected* of her.

One Step at a Time (First ... Then)

Teach the child that things happen in sequence. "First this, then that." Provide positive reinforcement or incentives for things that she has trouble completing (e.g., "First pick up your toys, then we can go for a walk."). You can also use the words "if ... then" (e.g., "If you get your homework done, then we can play a game.").

The Power to Choose

Transitions can be difficult because the child doesn't feel in control. If you think the child might protest a transition, provide a choice that will make him feel in greater control of the situation. For example, ask him if he wants to wear a sweater or a long-sleeve shirt to school instead of picking his clothes for him. To get him out the door in the morning, ask him if he wants to walk or skip to the car. To leave the park, ask if he wants one last swing or slide before leaving.

Toolbox of Calming Strategies

Use an old toolbox, or a plastic bin to represent a "toolbox," and fill it with "tools" (i.e., strategies) the child can use to help regulate emotions and solve problems during difficult transitions. Work together with the child to come up with tools she feels would be effective in calming her emotions. This may include a favorite stuffed animal, pictures of things/people, fidgets to squeeze, and visuals of how to take a deep breath, such as the Six Sides of Breathing; see visual on page 88. Remind the child that the toolbox is there to help her throughout the day when she experiences big emotions or problems or "fix."

Contributed by Leah Kuypers

HOLIDAYS AND SPECIAL EVENTS

GOVERNMENT

AND
NATIONAL
HOLIDAYS

Hidden Rules: 1. It is *unexpected* to talk about your views on certain political topics in certain settings. It's best to have these conversations with people you are very familiar with. 2. It's offensive to tell someone that they are wrong in their political or social beliefs.

Celebrating Presidents' Day

Use coins to talk about the presidents. Have the child pick a coin to determine which president is represented (e.g., Lincoln, Washington, Jefferson) and paste it to a piece of paper. Have him do research on when they were president, what they stood for, and what they are remembered for. Have him step into their shoes to try to feel what it might be like to be president back then or even today.

Model Citizen

Vote, obey the law, serve on a jury, volunteer, work towards change that you believe in and be nice to others. By being a model citizen you show the child what is important and how we work together for the greater good.

Job Talk: "Do you want to be a voter or volunteer worker?"

It Takes a Village

Help the child understand the concept that "it takes a village" and that people need to work together to keep our country running. Help her understand that she can work towards something that she believes in to make a difference and contribute to society and the welfare of others. For example, if she cares a lot about the environment, have her start a campaign at her school to celebrate Earth Day.

For the Love of Mom/Dad

Help the child brainstorm about what mom/dad might want as a gift for Mother's or Father's Day. Have her think about what her parents like and what makes them happy. This helps the child practice thinking of what others like and that we all have personal preferences and like to be thought about by others.

Queen or King for the Day

Help the child make a card letting mom/dad know how much he appreciates them and all that they do. Help him think of things he can do throughout the day that would make them happy, such as getting them a cup of tea or bringing them breakfast in bed.

Happy Helpers

Mom and dad love when children help out around the house, help with a younger sibling, or even just take care of themselves. With the child, make a list of the things she can do to help and turn it into coupons or a card that she can give on Mother's or Father's Day, such as taking out the garbage, walking the dog, folding the laundry, etc. See sample coupon on page 81.

Job Talk: "You be a bed maker, dog walker, dish washer (jobs to help mom and dad)."

MOTHER'S/ FATHER'S DAY

Hidden Rules 1. Giving a gift that is homemade is a special treat. It is a "thinking of others" gesture. 2. Families come in different shapes and sizes. Some have two homes, some have two moms or two dads or just one parent. It is important to be sensitive when talking about Mother's Day or Father's Day because some children don't have a "traditional" mother or father.

4TH OF JULY

Family Constitution

Take this time to talk about the history of the United States and what the 4th of July represents. Have family members review the Declaration of Independence and the U.S. Constitution/Bill of Rights and how running a family is similar to running a country. Discuss the importance of rules, and develop a family constitution that everyone can agree on and abide by (e.g., the right to privacy, the right to express your thoughts and opinions). Feel free to add other rules such as "pick up after yourself" or "talk nicely to others." Every family has different rules, and it is important to know what is expected.

What Do You Already Know?

Make *smart guesses* about what might happen on the 4th of July. Discuss what your family has done in past years (hindsight) and what you may do this year. Talk about who might be at the event and what might happen. Recalling the details and making predictions about what the child already knows is a great way to increase the use of hindsight and forethought (being able to use past experiences and future thinking). These are important skills for executive functioning. Will there be fireworks? A parade? What will be the same and what might be different?

Don't Be a Space Invader

When going to a parade, be aware that there will be a lot of people crowded into one place. Talk to the child about how to behave in a crowd, keeping her body to herself and trying not to lean or push on people around her. Let her know that touching others can make them feel uncomfortable.

Detective

Look at people in costumes or photos of people in costumes and help the child determine how they feel and what they might say (e.g., how does the witch feel and what does she say?). Encourage the child to use what she already knows about the characters to make *smart guesses* about their feelings and how they express themselves.

Ghouls and Goblins

After the child has chosen what he wants to be for Halloween, have him figure out what accessories that character might need and how he might act based on his knowledge of the character. Role-play how he will act when he is "in character" if he goes to a party or goes trick-or-treating.

Pumpkins Have Feelings, Too!

Carve pumpkins with various facial expressions. Have the child identify and then act out how the pumpkins might be feeling and what they might say, depending on how they look.

Job Talk: "Do you want be the carver? I'll be the scooper."

Trick-or-Treat

Role-play trick-or-treating with the child. Point out that it is a nice gesture when people give out candy and treats and that he must show appreciation by thanking them and treating them with respect. During the evening, take a break to rest and do a social autopsy about how the night is going. Praise the child for the things he is doing well such as, "I noticed you said thank you to the man who gave you that candy," and if he needs coaching, use this time to do so, "Let's try to keep up with everyone so that we can be part of the group." See page 87 for a sample social autopsy worksheet. As part of this activity (or once it's finished), refer to the mood meter (see page 72) and check in about how the child is feeling. If you don't have the mood meter nearby, ask him to describe how the activity made him feel.

Job Talk: "You be the bag holder/trick-or-treater."

HALLOWEEN

Hidden Rules: 1. If you say something mean about someone's costume (e.g., "I was that last year; that's for babies."), it will make them feel bad. 2. If offered a choice, take one piece of candy or treat from each house when trick-or-treating. 3. Usually, trick-or-treating starts when the sun goes down and ends before 9 pm. 4. If the light is not on at somebody's house, that usually means that they are not home or are not handing out candy, so don't knock or ring their doorbell.

THANKSGIVING

Hidden Rules: 1. Families give "thanks" in different ways. Some pray, some hold hands, and some make a short speech. When someone at the table gives "thanks," it is *expected* that you listen quietly (some people close their eyes and bow their head). 2. It is nice to help set the table and help clean up when there is a large family gathering. 3. It is nice to say "thank you" to the person who did the cooking for the day.

The History of Thanksgiving

Research the history of Thanksgiving and talk about what it would be like if you lived in those days. Step into the shoes of a pilgrim.

Job Talk: "You be the baker/chef."

Giving Thanks

Write a list of what you and the child are thankful for. Be sure to include the reasons why you are thankful for each other. Share this list with each other and the family. You can also do this activity verbally, maybe at the dinner table before or after the meal. Being thankful is a win-win situation – it makes the people you're showing thanks for feel good, and it helps to build positive thinking and awareness of the good things in the child's life.

Planning a Meal

Have the child help make part of the Thanksgiving dinner. Include him in reviewing the recipe, buying the ingredients, and sequencing the steps involved in cooking the meal. Make sure that he gets acknowledged for his hard work, maybe in front of the family when others can hear, such as "I'm grateful for Miguel's help with preparing this special meal." Positive experiences and praise build confidence. As part of this activity (or once it's finished), refer to the mood meter (see page 72) and check in about how the child is feeling. If you don't have the mood meter nearby, ask him to describe how the activity made him feel.

Giving Back

Make a family tradition of thinking about others who are less fortunate than you. Make a plan to visit a shelter, serve food to the homeless, or visit a nursing home to show that you care about others. Let the child choose how he would like to "give back" to others. This is a great opportunity for stepping into other people's shoes and being aware of and grateful for the things that you have.

Holiday Gift Giving

When thinking about what to buy people for the holidays, involve the child and have her look through magazines and make *smart guesses* about what each family member would like. If she has trouble thinking of a gift for somebody, have her interview them to find out what they would like. Gift giving is great for thinking of others and stepping into their shoes.

Charity Begins at Home

Make a family tradition of *thinking about others* over the holidays and donate a gift to a charity or give to someone in need. This will help the child develop perspective-taking skills.

Bigger Than a Breadbox

Have the child make *smart guesses* about what's in a gift before he opens it. If is it flat and square, could it be a book? Activities like this are great for inferencing and predicting.

Job Talk: "You be a guesser."

MAJOR HOLIDAYS

Teaching the Skills

Discuss, explain, and role-play in preparation for the various events that will take place over the holidays; for instance, sitting at the dinner table during several courses, waiting for others to open gifts, etc. It is important for the child to "add to the fun" of the holidays instead of "taking away from the fun." Knowing what is *expected* will help ensure that it happens.

Hidden Rules: 1. Not everyone celebrates the same holidays. Remember to be sensitive to other people's beliefs. 2. It is *unexpected* to tell somebody what you're giving them before they open the present. Be patient while others are opening their gifts so you don't spoil their enjoyment. 3. Holidays can be stressful for adults who have a lot of work to do to prepare, so try to be helpful or stay out of their way.

BIRTHDAY PARTIES

Shopping for Others

Have the child brainstorm about what the "birthday person" enjoys and likes. Go to the store while thinking of that person and pick out a gift that he would like. This is a great activity for thinking of others and building perspective taking.

Job Talk: "Be a thoughtful shopper!"

Thoughtful Words

Help the child make a birthday card for a friend, keeping in mind what color the friend likes and what type of stickers she might like on the card. Help the child write something nice or thank the person for inviting her to the birthday party.

Goodie Bags

Most children remember the last part of a social event the best. If they leave with a special treat or goodie bag, this helps create a positive memory about the party. Help the child decide what should go into the goodie bags by thinking about what her friends enjoy and what they might like to take home.

Pretend Party

Role-play the events that typically occur at a birthday party (e.g., playing games, unwrapping presents, blowing out candles, eating cake) to prepare the child for each situation. Set her up for success by priming her ahead of time.

Job Talk: "You be the wrapper/blower/eater."

Let the Party Begin!

When it is the child's birthday party, keep it small and try to come up with a few activities that will involve all the children who attend. Teach him how to do a *social fake* and have him practice keeping a neutral or happy face even when he doesn't like a gift or might already have a particular item that someone gave him, by saying "thank you" rather than "I already have that." Make sure that he thanks everyone for coming and tries to include each guest in the fun.

Helping the Host

When you have a dinner party or barbeque at your house, assign the child a role for helping out. Have him set the table, greet the guests, or clean up before or after the party. Help him to complete the assigned task by providing prompts or supports, and don't forget to praise him for helping out.

Job Talk: "You be the greeter/cleaner/ dish washer, etc."

Practice Makes Perfect

Let the child know what is *expected* during a particular gathering (e.g., being quiet at the table, playing by herself) and take time to role-play and practice before the guests come. Set realistic expectations and rules and make sure you are making it rewarding for her (e.g., she gets to watch a special movie with everyone after eating calmly at the dinner table).

Verbal Ping-Pong

Small-talk at parties is a type of verbal ping-pong in that it usually consists of back-and-forth questions and answers about what's new or what's going on at the party. Play conversation/small-talk ping-pong with the child to see how many verbal exchanges he can carry out about what's new, the food at the party, the weather, etc.

Party Tricks

Teach the child to do a trick with your dog or other pet or demonstrate something he has learned recently (e.g., reciting a poem or playing a tune on the piano). This can be a nice way to entertain guests at a party. Practice ahead of time and pick a special time for the performance. See sample kid tricks on page 89.

Job Talk: "Be a singer, joker, pianist."

DINNER PARTIES

Hidden Rules: 1. When guests come to your house, it is *expected* that you say "hello" and let them come in. 2. It's polite to compliment the host on the food that was served and say thanks for inviting you before you leave. 3. Ask to be excused from the dinner before leaving the table.

VACATION PLANNING AND ORGANIZING

Itinerary, Please!

Make sure to spell out to the child what's going to happen on your vacation. A schedule of the entire vacation plan is good so all family members know what is *expected*; in addition, a schedule of the daily events can help the child know what is happening throughout the day and reduce anxiety stemming from unfamiliar experiences, people, and transitions. A social narrative can be written and read prior to the vacation to set her up for success. Photos or drawings can also be used for a narrative. See sample on page 90.

Busy Minds

Use a map to show the child where you're going, how long it'll take, and when you'll be taking rest breaks. Let him have his own map so he can help and be the navigator, marking off places you have visited.

Job Talk: "Can you be the navigator?"

Tour Guide

When you arrive at your destination, have the child be the guide by reading the map, picking up brochures, and pointing out the different sites to see. This can build leadership and initiation skills.

Sticking to a Schedule

Although vacations typically don't follow a set routine, try to develop some sort of daily schedule to help the child understand, predict, and expect when it's time to eat, sleep, etc. If the schedule will change for a day, communicate that to her and have her help develop the new plan. Don't forget that healthy eating and sleep can help the child be a happy camper.

Job Talk: "You be a planner."

Hidden Rules: 1. When riding on a plane, keep your body to yourself. Use only one armrest; you're sharing a very small space. 2. Not everyone likes the same music. When you're in the car with other people, be flexible and listen to what others like to hear as well as what you like to listen to. 3. Sometimes airplanes don't run on schedule. Try to wait calmly and keep yourself occupied with a book, game, or music during the wait.

How Are They Connected?

If you're sitting by the pool, hanging out at the beach, or waiting for an airplane, play *social detective* games with the child such as "guess who belongs to whom." Watch people around you and try to decide who's related and belongs in the same family. For example, if two children are playing together and sitting with their parents, they are probably brother and sister. These *smart guesses* help build observation skills for understanding social situations and relationships.

Job Talk: "You be the detective/observer."

It's Nice to Be Nice!

If you're staying at a hotel or motel that has an elevator, have the child ask the people who come into the elevator with you which floor they are going to and if they would like her to push the button for them. Have her observe their faces to see how it makes them feel to be helped in this way. Refer to the mood meter (on page 72) to help her determine the feelings of others based on their facial expressions and nonverbal clues. Also, practice being a *social detective* in the elevator and make *smart guesses* about where the people might be going for the day based on what they are wearing or carrying. To the fitness room? Pool? On a hike? Out for dinner?

Job Talk: "You're the button pusher."

Hidden Rules: 1. Most of the friends you make on a short vacation will just be friends for that period of time. 2. Put your bathing suit on before you come out to the pool to swim and always wear sunscreen. 3. When on public transportation, it is *expected* that you use a quiet voice when talking. 4. At the pool, don't make comments out loud about other people's bodies. 5. Go to the bathroom before you get in the pool; it is unsanitary to pee in the pool. 6. There are chemicals in the pool that are not good for you to drink. Try to not swallow the water that you are swimming in.

Memories

With help as needed, have the child write in a journal about the high and low points of the vacation. Help him write a story to share with friends when you return. This is also great for conversation starters when spending time with friends. As part of this activity (or once it's finished), refer to the mood meter (see page 72) and check in about how the child is feeling. If you don't have the mood meter nearby, ask the child to describe how the activity made him feel.

Job Talk: "Be a journalist."

VACATION FUN

Document and Tell Stories

Be sure to take photos to document your trip. When you get back, put them in an album, review them with the child, and practice telling brief stories that she can tell to other people to share her experience.

New Places, New People

When you visit a new city or country, teach the child about the culture, living conditions, or way of life of the people who live there. Help him think about others and realize that other people live different lives than he does. This plants seeds of perspective taking.

"Say Cheese!"

Take pictures of the events you experience on your trip so that you can recall and discuss them with the child and others when you return. Try to capture people displaying various emotions. Later on, you and the child can make *smart guesses* about how they were feeling and why.

Job Talk: "I'll be the photographer and you be the smiler."

"Name That Tune" and Other Car Games

Play "Name That Tune." Have each person give clues about the song he or she is going to sing, including the name of the singer, the style of music, what show it is from, and the number of notes you are allowed to guess it. This is great for giving logical clues and making *smart guesses*. When going on family car vacations, be sure to bring other car games, such as "Bingo" or "20 Questions."

DON'T STOP NOW …

As a parent or caregiver, you have countless opportunities to teach and model social skills and social participation. Family life is filled with teachable moments. The hope is that this book will encourage you to make the most of these times, whether you're helping your child practice a skill, rehearsing for an upcoming event, or praising your child's appropriate behavior. Modify the activities in ways that make sense for your family and your child's learning style. You are the best judge of what works in navigating a path toward social success.

As you review the activities provided in this book, you'll likely recognize things you're already doing. Parents have good instincts about their children, and even if you haven't put a name to the strategies, you already understand many of the ways in which your child needs guidance. Take a moment to recognize all that you're already doing to support your child's social development and continue to create more opportunities to help the child thrive!

Strategies for Infusing Social/Emotional Learning Into Everyday Activities

Many evidence-based (i.e., backed by research) methods and philosophies are effective for helping children develop social competence, and it takes many years to gain expertise in all of those interventions. This book is not intended to turn parents into therapists or be overwhelming with too much information. However, an overview of several key terms and strategies is provided below to give an understanding of the methods most easily used at home. Please also refer to the Appendix, which lists articles, books, and other sources that provide evidence for the effectiveness of these strategies.

Teachable Moments

Teachable moments refer to taking advantage of everyday natural opportunities to provide insight, practice, and participation. Some evidence-based therapy practices use teachable moments to take advantage of the home, school, and community to create situations that will encourage learning and teach new skills for these environments (National Autism Center, 2011). For parents, these moments can be planned or unplanned. For example, while playing a board game, think about the opportunities that arise that can reinforce how to be a good sport. Also, if a child can't do something for himself, it can be a good opportunity to teach him how to ask for help.

These moments are perfect for working on awareness, skill building, and generalization of social skills. The spontaneous, natural environment provides hands-on coaching opportunities that can help the child understand how his behavior affects others and the outcome of a social situation. For example, if a child takes a toy from another child without asking and the other child is crying, we can use that opportunity to say "Oh no. I see that

he is crying because you took his toy from him. Can you give it back and ask him if you can play with it next time instead of taking it from him?" Life is full of teachable moments for parents to capture and take advantage of to support the child's social competence.

Modeling

Most children see and hear more than we give them credit for. They can be like parrots and "model" what they see and hear and, thus, purposefully or accidentally, learn by observing the behaviors of parents, siblings, peers, and teachers. This is why it is important to model the behaviors that we want our children to learn (National Autism Center, 2011). For example, we must do our best to be kind to others, use language that we would like our children to use, and avoid putting them in front of TV or other media that shows behavior or language that we don't want them to use. We can also be role models during play times and teachable moments. For example, when playing a board game, and you lost, say something like, "It's hard to lose, but I'm going to try to be a good sport and not get upset; it was fun anyway." Also, it's good for children to hear our positive self-talk so they can value the importance of internal encouragement and motivation. Show them that we all need an inner cheerleader to help us through life's hurdles. For example, when cooking, say something like, "Last time I made these cookies, they were not very moist. I think I'll put in less flour to see if I can make them taste better this time." And remember, nobody is perfect. So when you put your foot in your mouth or the child sees something that you don't think is a good social model, also use that as a teachable moment and show how to repair the situation, apologize, or do it differently. Use your own relationships, friendships, and social situations to be a good model for the child's social learning and development.

Social Briefing or Priming

We all feel more comfortable when we know what to expect or what we are supposed to do for a specific task or situation. Where we are going? How long will it last? Who will be there? What am I supposed to bring or do when I'm there? These are common questions for everybody. It is important to recognize that our children do better and are less anxious when they have an idea about what will happen in a given social situation. This will help set them up for success, feel more at ease, and possibly reduce challenging behaviors. We can do this by previewing information or activities that a child is likely to have difficulties with before the event happens. This is called priming (Aspy & Grossman, 2011; Koegel et al., 2003). This may be done by using a social narrative (Gray, 2000), which is a personalized story that describes a social situation (see page 90). It may be about what they should or should not do. Don't forget to talk about the hidden social rules. For example, "When you go to Johnny's house, his parents would like everyone to take off their shoes so the carpet does not get dirty."

Social Debriefing or Social Autopsy

Just as important as it is to talk about what will happen before it happens, it is important to talk about what happened after it happens. Discussing outcomes and debriefing about what went well and what could be done differently can be very helpful. Also referred to as a social autopsy (Lavoie, 2005) (see page 87), it involves reviewing and dissecting how a social situation went after it has happened. This strategy can be used to analyze and examine social interactions and behaviors that attributed to a positive or negative outcome such as after your son shared the ball with a peer at recess, the peer asked him if he could play after school.

When these behaviors are identified, he is more likely to repeat them again. Similar to social narratives, words, pictures, or cartoons may be used, or it may be done verbally with no writing involved. It's best done when the child is calm and focused, not during a time when the child is upset. Review what happened and what went well, discuss options of what could have been done better, and talk about alternative choices and problem solve for the future. This is also an excellent opportunity to practice taking into consideration and discussing how the other person might have felt (positively or negatively) in response to the child's actions, thereby building perspective-taking skills. It can be as simple as identifying and talking about how another person felt when the child gave him a birthday card (making him feel good) or blew out the birthday boy's candles on his birthday cake before he had the chance to do so himself (making him feel mad or sad). For example, "I could tell that Joey really liked the birthday card you made for him; that made him feel good. I also noticed that he seemed upset when you blew out his candles before he was able to blow them out. Did you notice that?" Taking the time to talk about situations before and after they happen (also called priming and debriefing) is an extremely effective way to promote generalization of the skills we are trying to build.

Play

Play is one of the most important ways by which children learn to be social. During play, children build language skills, sensory and motor skills, imagination, problem solving and planning skills, the ability to participate successfully, critical thinking, and social regulation. Play offers an avenue for parents and caregivers to engage and connect and provides many teachable moments for skill building and social/emotional growth. Facilitating opportunities for play with other children further supports developmental growth (Wolfberg, 2009) (see suggestions for setting up successful play dates on page 96). Play can take place anywhere and at any time, either during structured or unstructured time. Toys and objects can be used and selected that meet the development level and interest of the child. Try to engage the child by following her lead and wishes with regard to the type of play and sequence of activities (Greenspan, Wieder, & Simons, 2008). For example, if you are at the park and the child is playing in the sand, take off your shoes and get down to her level and play in the sand. If she is building a castle, build with her; if she is burying her feet in the sand, hide your feet, too. If other children are playing nearby, invite them to join in. Focus on the shared enjoyment of the moment rather than the product or outcome.

Prompting

Prompting involves giving children support, cues, or assistance to complete a task or give a desired response. There are various ways to prompt, such as *physical prompting* (helping the child build a tower by using your hand over her hand to pick up the blocks and stack them); *verbal prompting* (directly or indirectly stating what you would like the child to do, such as "say hello" – direct verbal – or "what do you need to say when you see someone?" – indirect verbal); *gestural prompting* (pointing or showing with your body/eyes what you would like the child to do); and *visual prompting* (showing the child exactly what you would like her to do by modeling, using photos, schedules, writing, or other visual cues) (Maurice, Green, & Luce, 1996).

It is important to provide enough support or prompting to help the child be successful and feel confident. At the same time, it is important to provide the least amount of prompting necessary so that the child can eventually act on her own without assistance. When thinking about the type of prompting to provide, from most to least, it is helpful to understand the difference between declarative language and imperative language.

Declarative language explains or refers to the desired outcome without telling the child exactly what to do so he can accomplish what needs to be done on his own and develop the ability to use self-talk as his own internal coach. This enables him to initiate tasks to complete a goal without direct verbal prompting or coaching from an adult. For example, "Hmm, I see dirty dishes on the table" or "Your hands look dirty." This type of thinking builds self-monitoring, problem solving, and overall metacognition – the awareness of one's own thinking and learning. *Imperative language*, on the other hand, is a command or a direct verbal prompt that tells someone exactly what to do. For example, "Put your dirty dishes in the sink" or "Wash your hands." The latter prompting type does not allow the child to problem solve and think for himself and, therefore, does not foster independence and self-help capabilities.

Supporting Emotions

Being aware of one's emotions and being able to regulate or control them is essential for social success. If we are unable to manage our emotional state and/or overt behaviors to adapt to various social demands, we will have minimal success in social situations. When our emotions and behaviors don't match the social situation, it makes others feel uncomfortable and not want to be around us. For example, if a child continues to run around the classroom after recess and struggles to calm down, the teacher and the other students become frustrated and possibly upset, which might result in the child being sent out of the class. When children struggle to manage their emotions on a regular basis, sometimes labels such as *hyper, impulsive, lazy, disruptive, noncompliant*, etc., are used. These labels may point to a deficit in social regulation, and it's important to figure out the root of the problem and what area(s) the child needs help with in order to build their skills and help them be more successful.

Similar to emotional regulation, Daniel Goleman (1995) maintains that **emotional intelligence** (EQ) is more important than IQ (intelligence quotient) because it affects more of the foundational skills that help us understand relationships and acquire leadership and self-management skills. If emotional regulation skills are lagging, it is difficult to focus on learning and relating to others effectively. When a child has a high EQ, he is able to regulate himself and stay focused and calm, allowing him to attend to important academic skills and challenges. When a child is having trouble with EQ or social regulation, on the other hand, he may struggle with the classroom, school, and academic demands.

Goleman suggests that parents become emotional coaches and use real-life emotional moments and situations as teachable moments to help children understand their own feelings as well as the feelings of others. In order to do this, parents need to watch and check in with their children and their teachers. This will help them recognize when the child is having an emotional reaction to a situation where coaching might help. If a child seems to be sad or upset on a regular basis after recess, for example, she might need some emotion coaching to talk about her feelings and determine what is going on at recess that is upsetting her. When emotions are too volatile, sometimes kids need time to calm down or reflect before they can think clearly and learn from or work through a situation.

As caregivers, it is important for us to listen with full attention and acknowledge the child's feelings so that she feels heard and understood. For example, when the child is mad about something, get down to her level (e.g., bend down and make eye contact), listen to what happened, and say something like, "That sounds frustrating." This can help calm the child down and become able to problem solve. Later, when the child is in the state of mind to process her emotions, parents can help provide language and la-bel the feelings with emotion words (e.g., "you must have felt mad" or "your face looks sad right now"). Then problem solving can occur either naturally through conversation, drawing, or writing or with a little prompting (outlined above) and role-play (outlined on pages 57-58).

Lastly, we cannot overlook the importance of keeping the brain emotionally regulated and primed for learning by making sure children get enough sleep, hydration, and proper nutrition. Without enough sleep, kids cannot think clearly, and their behavior may reflect an inability to process emotions and make good choices. Food is our body's fuel, and water is a mood regulator. Make sure to provide enough healthy protein and fat and drink at least eight glasses of water a day. Similar to gasoline for a car and water for plants, we need to make sure children get the proper ingredients to fuel their brain function and be able to perform a healthy daily "social diet."

Reinforcement and Praise

We are continuously telling kids how to do things or what *not* to do. It is important to pay attention to what they're doing well and provide feedback during those specific moments. Catch the child trying hard at something or doing something that is helpful or nice to others. Acknowledge the child's positive behavior by praising her with words or gestures, which in most cases will validate the child and increase her drive to repeat these desired behaviors.

When verbally praising a child, it is important to acknowledge the child for effort, hard work, and willingness to try (e.g., "I can see you're taking your time decorating that cake; it looks great" or "Wow, you didn't give up!"). This supports a growth mindset (Dweck, 2006) and intrinsic motivation to feel good about doing your best job. The opposite consists of praising the child's natural abilities such as intelligence (e.g., "you're so smart"), which creates a fixed mindset and can result in children not focusing on hard work and getting stuck if they think something might be too difficult.

Taking this strategy a step further, Sarah Ward, speech-language pathologist and expert in executive functioning, recommends praising the **action** and **outcome** along with an **exclamation** to increase the child's awareness of the future and reason for the task (personal communication, 2013). For example, rather than using global statements such as "good job," which doesn't help the child understand why the task was important, say, "Wow, thanks for hanging up your towel (action). Now it can dry on the rack (outcome). Cool (exclamation)."

The ultimate goal is to build intrinsic motivation so that children don't need extrinsic or material items as a driving force to do well. However, when this presents as a challenge and verbal praise or natural social rewards, such as a smile or intrinsically feeling good about the behavior, is not motivating the child, rewards or reinforcers can be tried. This strategy is based on the principles of applied behavior analysis (ABA). According to the tenets of ABA, behavior that is followed by a reinforcing consequence is more likely to happen again (Maurice et al., 1996).

It is important to realize that the same type of reinforcement doesn't work for all children. For example, one child may love hugs whereas another child finds that kind of closeness annoying. Therefore, it is important to assess what reinforcers work for each child through observation or asking directly. For many, a written checklist, also called a reinforcement menu (Aspy & Grossman, 2011; Rathvon, 2008), is a helpful tool. That is, from a list of possible reinforcers, the child checks off what he prefers (see a sample menu on page 91). Please note that preferences change, so review the menu, as needed. When a child develops more skills and/or intrinsic

motivation, be sure to taper off the tangible rewards or reinforcers so that he doesn't become dependent on them to perform or complete the task. The thought is that by providing positive praise or reinforcers for positive behavior, more desired behaviors will be nurtured and grow. This type of feedback can increase motivation and self-confidence. It can also help the child understand what it "feels like" to be successful and build a positive social memory tied to that desired behavior, and thus increase the motivation to perform the behavior again.

Role-Play/Rehearsal

Role-play, and also rehearsing – a part of role-play – gives children an opportunity to act out real-life situations to problem solve and practice social skills and build an image of what something might look like or feel like when it actually happens (Sohn & Crayson, 2005). For example, you can say, "Let's pretend you're at recess and someone bumps into you ..." Then act out what the child can do with her words, body, and behavior to manage the social situation. This provides an opportunity to find out how the child perceives various social situations and talk about how she feels going into a situation. You can also gain insight into what others are thinking/feeling. This type of practice can help with understanding and reading nonverbal cues as well as thinking of what to say and not to say in a situation. Role-plays can be used for practice working in a group, joining in play, having a conversation, or prepping for a job interview as the child gets older. By thinking about the situation and acting it out, various options can be developed and practiced to build self-esteem and confidence and promote positive social behaviors.

Job Talk

An interesting study (Bryan, Dweck, Rogers, & Walton, 2011) showed that people were more likely to turn out to vote if they were given the title of a "voter" vs. being told simply to "vote." This change in phrasing from a verb

("vote") to a noun ("voter") significantly increased the interest in action and, in turn, voter turnout! Bryan and colleagues suspect that this is due to how people view themselves as voters, something that is viewed as positive because it implies independence and self-determination versus just being told what to do.

Ward and Jacobsen (2012) applied this research to their work with children, translating it into a simple strategy that they call "job talk." Through clinical observations, they noticed increased motivation to complete a task by adding "-er" to action words. That is, turning a task or action into a "job" and adding "-er" gives the child a job title such as washer, wiper, toothbrusher, listener, etc. Manipulating the verb form of a behavior ("Annie, brush your teeth, please") to feature a noun label (Annie is a toothbrusher!)

creates an essential part of one's identity. In other words, it creates confidence and a positive sense of self – this is "What I can do!" This subtle shift in language can change an occasional behavior of helping around the house ("Please, set the table.") into a child who has confidence in her permanent trait or skill ("I am a tablesetter!"). Below are some examples.

Action/Verb Form	Noun/"Job Talk" Form
Wash your hands.	Can you be a handwasher?
Please wipe the counter off.	Be a counter wiper.
It's time to go upstairs and brush your teeth.	Time to be a toothbrusher!
Please take out your homework and start your math.	You're getting ready to be a mathematician.

Chart of All Activities and the Areas They Reinforce

This chart organizes and categorizes the activities in the book into the various areas of social regulation emphasized. Every activity supports a wide range of skills that cannot be covered in a single list. However, the following reflects the most prominent area(s) that each activity supports.

	Page	Emotional Regulation	Cognitive Flexibility	Nonverbal Language	Thinking of Others/ Perspective Taking	Expressive Language	Receptive Language & Following Directions	Imagination & Play	Executive Functioning	Social Rules	Observation & Social Awareness
AT HOME	9										
Mood Meter	10	X				X					X
Plan of the Day	10	X	X						X		
Match the Picture	10								X		X
Rain or Shine?	11								X		X
Planning Ahead	11	X							X		
Need a Pick-Me-Up?	11	X									
What to Wear?	11								X		X
Making Dinner Together	12								X		
Food for Thought: What's for Dinner?	12			X							X
Formal Dinners	12									X	X
Where Did It Come From?	12				X						
Review the Rules	13				X			X		X	
When All Else Fails, Vote!	13	X	X					X			
Play Nice and Add to the Fun	13		X		X			X		X	
Fair Play	13		X					X		X	
Following Someone Else's Plan	13		X		X			X			
Special Space	14							X		X	
Special Time	14		X					X		X	
Play Routines	14							X		X	
Have Fun!	14				X			X			
Dress-Up	15				X			X			
Building a Fort	15					X		X	X		
Boxes, Boxes, and More Boxes	15		X		X			X			
Write It Out, Act It Out	15		X	X		X		X			
Role-Play	15	X		X	X			X		X	

	Page	Emotional Regulation	Cognitive Flexibility	Nonverbal Language	Thinking of Others/ Perspective Taking	Expressive Language	Receptive Language & Following Directions	Imagination & Play	Executive Functioning	Social Rules	Observation & Social Awareness
Fun With Balloons	16		X	X							
Cooking up Some Fun	16				X	X					
Copycat	16			X		X					X
Nonverbal Games	16			X	X						X
Scavenger Hunt	16						X				X
Freeze Dance	16	X	X	X	X						
Place Setting	17				X				X		X
Anything Can Be Turned Into Fun and Gains!	17					X	X				X
Vacuuming	17			X			X				X
Whose Clothes?	17				X						X
Clear Vision for a Clean Future	17								X		X
What's in a Name?	18				X						X
Animals Help Cope With Emotions	18	X				X					
Caring for Pets = Building Responsibility	18				X		X		X		
Old Dog, New Tricks	18			X		X					
Emotional Benefits	18	X		X	X						
Receiving a Call	19					X	X			X	
Don't Be an Interruptosaurus!	19				X					X	X
Talking on the Phone	19				X		X			X	
Hand Signals	19			X						X	
Be a Family Detective	20				X						X
Teaching Social Skills Through Media	20			X	X						X
I See What You're Thinking	20		X	X							X
Who Gets to Pick?	20		X		X						
Learning the Characters	20				X						X
Reading the Visual Cues	20			X	X						X
A Picture Is Worth a Thousand Words	21			X							X
Thinking About the Family	21				X	X					
Emotions Scrapbooking	21	X		X							X
Family Tree	21				X						
I Think I'm Thinking	21			X						X	X

	Page	Emotional Regulation	Cognitive Flexibility	Nonverbal Language	Thinking of Others/ Perspective Taking	Expressive Language	Receptive Language & Following Directions	Imagination & Play	Executive Functioning	Social Rules	Observation & Social Awareness
Comic Relief	22				X	X				X	
Family Skits	22			X	X			X			
Talent Show	22				X	X	X		X		
Best in Show	22			X	X						
Charades	22	X		X				X			X
Talent Comes in All Shapes and Sizes	22				X	X					
Handmade Thoughts	23				X	X					X
Visualizing With the End in Mind	23							X	X		
The Original Paper Doll	23	X		X							X
Inside Others' Minds	23				X						X
Drawing – Snapshot of a Child's Point of View	23				X	X					
Pen Pals	23				X	X					
Service With a Smile	24				X	X			X		
1. Get Ready, 2. Do, 3. Done	24								X		
Social Contagion – The Domino Effect	24			X	X						
Surprise Snack	24			X	X						
Eyes Have Thoughts	24		X	X	X		X	X			X
Talking Stick	25	X				X					
Wonder Questions	25				X	X					
Dinner Schedule	25								X		
Conversation Cards	25					X	X		X		
Table Manners	25								X		X
"Eye See You"	25			X	X						X
Show and Tell	25					X	X				
How Was Your Day?	26	X			X	X					
Observing Acts of Kindness	26				X						X
Nighttime Routine	26	X	X								X
Sweet Dreams	26					X					
Calming Strategies – Winding Down	26	X									
Gratitude	26				X						

	Page	Emotional Regulation	Cognitive Flexibility	Nonverbal Language	Thinking of Others/ Perspective Taking	Expressive Language	Receptive Language & Following Directions	Imagination & Play	Executive Functioning	Social Rules	Observation & Social Awareness
Scrubbing Is Loving	27				X				X		
Follow the Steps	27						X		X		
Mirror, Mirror	27	X									X
Make a Splash	27							X			
Stepping Into the Character's Shoes	28				X						
Listening With the Whole Body	28	X								X	
Reading/Literacy	28	X			X						
Wordless Picture Books	28				X	X			X		X
Guessing What the Book Is About	28				X			X			X
Story Telling	28					X					
Finishing the Story	28					X	X				
IN THE COMMUNITY	29										
Set the Child up for Success – "Priming"	30	X			X					X	X
Debriefing	30	X			X					X	
Same But Different	30	X	X						X		
"I Spy . . ."	30				X						X
Would You Rather?	31				X	X		X			
B.I.N.G.O. Was His Name – O	31				X						X
Guess the Destination	31				X						X
Share Your Feelings	31	X				X					
Time to Listen	31					X					
Why Are We Here?	32				X						X
What's My Perspective	32		X	X							X
Asking for Help	32					X	X		X		
"Do You See What I See?"	32				X						X
Coping with Emotions	32	X									
"Hold the Door, Please"	32			X	X						X
Sharing Is Caring	33		X		X			X			
Snow or Sand Trails	33				X						X
Choosing Friends	33				X						X
Social Exposure	33	X						X		X	X
Sharing Your Imagination	33		X			X		X			
Partner and Group Activities	33		X		X		X	X			

	Page	Emotional Regulation	Cognitive Flexibility	Nonverbal Language	Thinking of Others/ Perspective Taking	Expressive Language	Receptive Language & Following Directions	Imagination & Play	Executive Functioning	Social Rules	Observation & Social Awareness
Grocery List	34								X		
What Aisle?	34								X		X
Helping Hands	34				X						X
Food Routes – Connect the Dots!	34				X						
Step by Step	35		X						X		
What Are You Going to Have?	35				X						X
Social Spying	35				X						X
Chef for the Day	35				X						
Validating Feelings	36	X									
Do a Practice Run	36	X							X	X	
Analyzing Ads	36				X						X
Guessing Your Stats	36										X
Preshow	37				X				X		
Quiet in the Theater	37				X					X	
Post-Show	37					X					
The Spotlight's on You	37				X	X					
Exploring Your World	38					X					X
Pay It Forward	38				X						
Who Are the People in Your Neighborhood?	38				X						X
Friendly Greetings	38			X	X	X				X	
Safety First – Don't Talk to Strangers	38									X	X
Playing Ball	39		X				X			X	
Watching Sports	39									X	
Building Emotional Vocabulary Can Be a Sport in Itself!	39	X								X	
Hidden Rules Change From Situation to Situation	40									X	X
Life Happens	40	X	X								
One Step at a Time (First … Then)	40								X	X	
The Power to Choose	40	X									
Toolbox of Calming Strategies	40	X									

	Page	Emotional Regulation	Cognitive Flexibility	Nonverbal Language	Thinking of Others/ Perspective Taking	Expressive Language	Receptive Language & Following Directions	Imagination & Play	Executive Functioning	Social Rules	Observation & Social Awareness
HOLIDAYS AND SPECIAL EVENTS	41										
It Takes a Village	42				X						X
Model Citizen	42										
Celebrating Presidents' Day	42				X				X		
For the Love of Mom/Dad	43				X						X
Queen or King for the Day	43				X						X
Happy Helpers	43				X				X		
Don't Be a Space Invader	44				X					X	X
What Do You Already Know?	44								X		
Family Constitution	44								X		
Detective	45	X		X							X
Pumpkins Have Feelings, Too!	45	X		X	X						
Ghouls and Goblins	45				X	X					
Trick-or-Treat	45				X				X		
Giving Back	46				X						
Planning a Meal	46								X		
Giving Thanks	46	X			X						
The History of Thanksgiving	46				X						
Holiday Gift Giving	47				X						X
Charity Begins at Home	47				X						
Bigger Than a Breadbox	47								X		X
Teaching the Skills	47								X		
Shopping for Others	48				X						X
Goodie Bags	48				X						
Thoughtful Words	48				X					X	
Pretend Party	48		X							X	
Let the Party Begin!	48				X	X				X	
Helping the Host	49				X				X		
Practice Makes Perfect	49									X	
Verbal Ping-Pong	49				X	X					
Party Tricks	49			X		X					

	Page	Emotional Regulation	Cognitive Flexibility	Nonverbal Language	Thinking of Others/ Perspective Taking	Expressive Language	Receptive Language & Following Directions	Imagination & Play	Executive Functioning	Social Rules	Observation & Social Awareness
Itinerary, Please!	50		X							X	
Busy Minds	50		X						X	X	
Tour Guide	50								X	X	
Sticking to a Schedule	50								X		
How Are They Connected?	51			X							X
It's Nice to Be Nice!	51			X	X						
Memories	51					X					
Document and Tell Stories	51					X					
New Places, New People	51				X						
Say Cheese!	51			X		X					
"Name That Tune" and Other Car Games	51					X					

References and Recommended Reading

Aspy, R., & Grossman, B. G. (2011). The Ziggurat Model: Release 2.0. A framework for designing comprehensive interventions for high-functioning individuals with autism spectrum disorders. Shawnee Mission, KS: AAPC Publishing.

Atwood, T. (1998). Asperger's syndrome: A guide for parents and professionals. Philadelphia, PA: Jessica Kingsley Publishers Limited (USA).

Ayres, A. J. (2005). Sensory integration and the child. Los Angeles, CA: Western Psychological Services.

Baron-Cohen, S. (1995). Mindblindness: An essay on autism and theory of mind. Cambridge, MA: The MIT Press.

Baron-Cohen, S., Leslie, A., & Frith, U. (1985). Does the autistic child have a "theory of mind"? Cognition, 21, 37-46.

Barry, T. D., Klinger, L. G., Lee, J. M., Palardy, N., Gilmore, T., & Bodin, S. D. (2003). Examining the effectiveness of an outpatient clinic social skills group for high-functioning children with autism. Journal of Autism and Developmental Disorders, 33(6), 685-701.

Blair, C. (2002). School readiness: Integrating cognition and emotion in a neurobiological conceptualization of children's functioning at school entry. American Psychologist, 57(2), 111-127.

Bodrova, E., & Leong, D. J. (2005). Self-regulation as a key to school readiness: How can early childhood teachers promote this critical competence? In M. Zaslow & I. Martinez-Beck (Eds.), Critical issues in early childhood professional development (section III). Baltimore, MD: Paul H. Brookes Publishing.

Bodrova, E., & Leong, D. J. (2007). Tools of the mind: The Vygotskian approach to early childhood education (2nd ed.). New York: Prentice-Hall.

Bolick, T. (2001). Asperger Syndrome and adolescence: Helping preteens and teens get ready for the real world. Gloucester, MA: Fair Winds Press.

Bronson, M. B. 2000. Self-regulation in early childhood: Nature and nurture. New York, NY: Guilford.

Bryan, C. J., Dweck, C. S., Rogers, T., & Walton, M. (2011). Motivating voter turnout by motivating the self. Proceedings of the National Academy of Sciences, 108(31), 12653-12656.

Buron, K. D., & Curtis, M. (2012). The incredible 5-point scale. Shawnee Mission, KS: AAPC Publishing.

Buron, K., & Wolfberg, P. (2008). Learners on the autism spectrum, preparing highly qualified educators. Shawnee Mission, KS: AAPC Publishing.

Cox, A. J. (2007). No mind left behind: Understanding and fostering executive control—the eight essential brain skills every child needs to thrive. New York, NY: Penguin Group (USA), Inc.

Dawson, P., & Guare, R. (2010). Executive skills in children & adolescents (2nd ed.). New York, NY: Guilford Publications.

Diamond, S. (2011). Social rules for kids: The top 100 social rules kids need to succeed. Shawnee Mission, KS: AAPC Publishing.

Dweck, C. (2006). Mindset. New York, NY: Random House.

Elman, N. M., & Kennedy-Moore, E. (2003). Unwritten rules of friendship: Simple strategies to help the child make friends. Boston, MA: Little, Brown, & Co.

Faber, A., & Mazlish, E. (1980). How to talk so kids will listen and listen so kids will talk. New York, NY: Rawson, Wade Publishers, Inc.

Gelman, S. A., & Heyman, G. D. (1999). Carrot-eaters and creature-believers: The effects of lexicalization on children's inferences about social categories. Psychological Science, 10(6), 489-493.

Gillespie, L., & Seibel, N. (2006). Self-regulation: A cornerstone of early childhood development. Beyond the Journal: Young Children on the Web. Retrieved from http://journal.naeyc.org/btj/200607/Gillespie709BTJ.pdf

Goldstein, H, Kaczmarek, L. A., & English, K. M. (2002). Promoting social communication: Children with developmental disabilities from birth to adolescence. Baltimore, MD: Paul H. Brookes Publishing Co.

Goleman, D. (1995). Emotional intelligence: Why it can matter more than IQ (10th anniversary ed.). New York, NY: Bantam, Random House, Inc.

Grau, V., & Whitebread, D. (2012). Self and social regulation of learning during collaborative activities in the classroom: The interplay of individual and group cognition. Learning and Instruction, 22(6), 401-412.

Gray, C. (2000). *The new Social Story™ book*. Arlington, TX: Future Horizons, Inc.

Greene, R. (1999). *The explosive child*. New York, NY: HarperCollins.

Greenspan, S., with Salmon, J. (1994). *Playground politics: Understanding the emotional life of your school-age child*. Redding, MA: Perseus Books.

Greenspan, S. L., Wieder, S. , & Simons, R. (2008). *The child with special needs: Encouraging intellectual and emotional growth*. Reading, MA: Addison-Wesley.

Gruber, R., Cassoff, J., Frenette, S., Wiebe, S., & Carrier, J. (2012). The impact of sleep extension and restriction on children's emotional liability and impulsivity. *Pediatrics, 130* (5), e1155-e1161. doi: 10.1542/peds.2012-0564

Heyman, G. (2008). Talking about success: Implications for achievement motivation. *Journal of Applied Developmental Psychology, 29*(5), 361-370.

Jacobsen P. (2005). *Understanding how Asperger children and adolescents think and learn*. London, UK, and Philadelphia, PA: Jessica Kingsley Publishers.

Koegel, L. K., Koegel, R. L., Frea, W., & Green-Hopkins, I. (2003). Priming as a method of coordinating educational services for students with autism. *Language, Speech, and Hearing Services in Schools, 34,* 228-235.

Koegel, L., Matos-Fredeen, R., Lang, R., & Koegel, R. (2011). Interventions for children with autism spectrum disorders in inclusive school settings. *Cognitive and Behavioral Practice,* CBPRA-00350. doi:10.1016/j.cbpra.2010.11.003

Kuypers, L. M. (2008). *The zones of regulation*. San Jose, CA: Social Thinking Publishing.

Kuypers, L., & Sautter, E. (2012, May-June). How to promote social regulation. *Autism Bay Area Magazine*, pp. 8-9.

Lantieri, L. (2008). *Building emotional intelligence: Techniques to cultivate inner strength in children*. Boulder, CO: Sounds True, Inc.

Levine, M. (2012). *Teach your children well: Parenting for authentic success*. New York, NY: HarperCollins.

Levine, M. D. (2002). *A mind at a time*. New York, NY: Simon & Schuster.

Lavoie, R. (2005). *It's so much work to be your friend: Helping the child with learning disabilities find social success*. New York, NY: Simon & Schuster.

Lavoie, R. (2005). Social skill autopsies: A strategy to promote and develop social competencies. *LDonline*. Retrieved from http://www.ldonline.org/article/14910/

MacDuff, G., Krantz, P., & McClannahan, L. (2001). Prompts and prompt-fading strategies for people with autism. In C. Maurice, G. Green, & R. M. Foxx (Eds.), *Making a difference: Behavioral intervention for autism* (pp. 37-50). Austin, TX: Pro-Ed.

Madrigal, S., & Winner, M. G. (2008). *Superflex: A superhero social thinking curriculum*. San Jose, CA: Social Thinking Publishing.

Maurice, C., Green, G., & Luce, S. C. (Eds.). (1996). *Behavioral intervention for young children with autism: A manual for parents and professionals*. Austin, TX: Pro-Ed, Inc.

McAfee, J. (2002). *Navigating the social world*. Arlington, TX: Future Horizons, Inc.

McClelland, M. M., Ponitz, C. C., Messersmith, E. E., & Tominey, S. (2010). Self-regulation: The integration of cognition and emotion. In R. Lerner (Series Ed.) & W. Overton (Vol. Ed.), *Handbook of lifespan human development, Vol. 4. Cognition, biology, and methods* (pp. 509–553). Hoboken, NJ: Wiley.

McCurry, C. (2009). *Parenting your anxious child with mindfulness and acceptance: A powerful new approach to overcoming fear, panic, and worry using acceptance and commitment therapy*. Oakland, CA: New Harbinger Publications, Inc.

Miller, C. (2006). Developmental relationships between language and theory of mind. *American Journal of Speech-Language Pathology, 15*, 142-154.

Myles, B. S., Trautman, M. L. , & Schelvan, R. L. (2013). *The hidden curriculum for understanding unstated rules in social situations for adolescents and young adults* (2nd ed.). Shawnee Mission, KS: AAPC Publishing.

Myles, J. M., & Kolar, A. (2013). *The hidden curriculum and other everyday challenges for elementary-age children with high-functioning autism*. Shawnee Mission, KS: AAPC Publishing.

National Autism Center. (2011). *A parent's guide to evidence-based practice and autism*. Retrieved from http://www.nationalautismcenter.org/learning/parent_manual.php

Ozonoff, S., Dawson, J., & McPartland, J. (2002). *A parent's guide to Asperger syndrome and high-functioning autism*. New York, NY: The Guilford Press.

Patrick, H. (1997). Social self-regulation: Exploring the relations between children's social relationships, academic self-regulation, and school performance. *Educational Psychologist, 32*(4), 209-220.

Prizant, B., Wetherby, A., Rubin, E., Laurent, A., & Rydell, P. (2007). *The SCERTS® model: A comprehensive educational approach for children with autism spectrum disorders* . Baltimore, MD: Brookes Publishing.

Quill, K. (Ed.). (1995). *Teaching children with autism: Strategies to enhance communication and socialization*. Albany, NY: Delmar.

Rapee, R., Wignall, A., Spence, S., Cobham, V., & Lyneham, H. (2000). *Helping your anxious child*. Oakland, CA: New Harbinger Publications, Inc.

Rathvon, N. (2008). *Effective school interventions: Evidence-based strategies for improving student outcomes*. New York, NY: The Guilford Press.

Sautter, E., & Wilson, K. (2011). *Whole body listening Larry at home*. San Jose, CA: Social Thinking Publishing.

Sautter, E., & Wilson, K. (2011). *Whole body listening Larry at school*. San Jose, CA: Social Thinking Publishing.

Shonkoff, J., & Phillips, D. (2000). *From neurons to neighborhoods: The science of early childhood development*. Washington, DC: National Academies Press.

Siegel, D. I., & Bryson T. (2011). *The whole-brain child: 12 revolutionary strategies to nurture your child's developing mind, survive everyday parenting struggles, and help your family thrive*. New York, NY: The Random House Publishing Company.

Sohn, A., & Grayson, C. (2005). *Parenting your Asperger child: Individualized solutions for teaching the child practical skills*. New York, NY: Penguin Group (USA), Inc.

Stewart, K. K., Carr, J. E., & LeBlanc, L. A. (2007). Evaluation of family-implemented behavioral skills training for teaching social skills to a child with Asperger's Disorder. *Clinical Case Studies, 6*(3), 252-262.

Truesdale, S. P. (1990). Whole body listening: Developing active auditory skills. *Language, Speech, and Hearing Services in Schools, 23*, 183-184.

Vagin, A. (2012). *Movie time social learning*. San Jose, CA: Social Thinking Publishing.

Vermeulen, P. (2013). *Autism as context blindness* (textbook ed.). Shawnee Mission, KS: AAPC Publishing.

Volet, S., Vauras, M., & Salonen, P. (2009). Self- and social regulation in learning contexts: An integrative perspective. *Educational Psychologist, 44*(4), 215-226.

Ward, S. (2013). *Practical strategies to improve executive function skills*. Presentation at Communication Works and the annual Social Thinking Provider's Conference, San Francisco, CA.

Ward, S., & Jacobsen, K. (2012). *Cognitive connections*. Concord, MA: Executive Function Practice.

Winner, M. G. (2000). *Inside out: What makes a person with social cognitive deficits tick*. San Jose, CA: Social Thinking Publishing.

Winner, M. G. (2005). *Think social! A social thinking curriculum for school-age students*. San Jose, CA: Social Thinking Publishing.

Winner, M. G. (2007). *Thinking about YOU thinking about ME*. San Jose, CA: Social Thinking Publishing.

Winner, M. G. (2008). *A politically incorrect look at evidence-based practices and teaching social skills*. San Jose, CA: Social Thinking Publishing.

Wolfberg, P. (2003). *Peer play and the autism spectrum: The art of guiding children's socialization and imagination*. Shawnee Mission, KS: AAPC Publishing.

Wolfberg, P. J. (2009). *Play and imagination in children with autism* (2nd ed.). New York, NY: Columbia, Teachers College Press.

Appendix

Vocabulary

Vocabulary designated by *italics* throughout the book is part of the Social Thinking Vocabulary developed by Michelle G. Winner, www.socialthink-ing.com. Used with permission.

Adding to the Fun/Taking Away From the Fun: Adding to the fun is do-ing anything that encourages children to play together and have a good time. Taking away from the fun is doing things that might make others feel bad or not want to play together.

Doing What Is "Expected": Understanding that a range of rules (stated or unstated – "hidden") exists in every situation and that we are responsible for figuring out what those rules are, and then following them by adapt-ing our words and/or behavior. By doing what is expected, we keep other people thinking good thoughts about us. Using the terms "expected/unexpected" rather than "good/bad" or "right/wrong," we remove subjec-tivity and demonstrate that what is "good" in one situation may be "bad" in another.

Doing What Is "Unexpected": Failing to follow the set of social rules, hid-den or stated, in the environment. When you do what is unexpected, peo-ple may have confused/unfriendly/grumpy/mad thoughts about you.

Flexible Thinking/Flexible Brain: Using mental flexibility to interpret ver-bal and nonverbal information based on different points of view or differ-ent contexts. Being able to "go with the flow" and "see the shades of gray," This is the opposite of having a rigid or "rock brain," where one follows a rule all the time or gets stuck on one's own ideas or desires.

Following the Plan/Following the Group Plan: Understanding that when in the presence of others, we work together to accomplish a com-mon goal, with all members thinking about the same plan. This involves taking into consideration what people are planning to do next based on their physical actions. We can also start to figure out what people are plan-ning to do by interpreting the subtle meanings of their language; this is a higher-level skill.

Interruptosaurus: A silly name for someone who interrupts when others are talking.

Keeping Your Brain and Body in the Group: To participate effectively within a group, our brains need to keep thinking about what the group is thinking (a topic, a lesson, an action, etc.); and our bodies (eyes, head, shoulders) need to be situated in a manner that shows we are interested and connected to the group.

Perspective Taking: Understanding that other people have thoughts, feelings, beliefs or experiences that might be different from ours.

Plan B: A second choice or plan for when unexpected situations occur.

Sharing Imagination: Being able to share your thoughts and ideas that you think about and imagine with another person. This is a large part of play and conversation.

Smart Guess: Taking information you already know or have been taught and making an educated guess about something using that information.

Social Autopsy/Social Debriefing: Talking about or dissecting a social situation after it's done (Lavoie, 2005). This helps to understand what hap-pened and determine what went well and what could be done differently next time.

Social Briefing/Priming: Explaining and outlining what is going to hap-pen during an upcoming event or social situation. This helps prepare the child for what to expect.

Social Detective: Looking at and thinking about the situation and the people in context. This includes using your eyes, ears, and brain to look for clues in the situation (the context) and from people to help determine what their plan might be or what they are thinking about.

Social Fake: Demonstrating interest in someone else's topic even if you don't find it all that fascinating. We use the social fake during boring moments to keep people feeling good about being around us. This requires focused and friendly facial expressions, eye contact, supportive words and gestures, etc.

Space Invader: Someone who gets too close to or invades another person's personal space. This shows the person is not thinking about others and what makes them feel comfortable/uncomfortable.

Thinking With Your Eyes: Using your eyes to interpret a situation and the nonverbal messages others are sending as well as to show others you are thinking about them.

Whole Body Listening (Truesdale, 1990): This concept teaches that listening is not just hearing with your ears but using your eyes (to look at the speaker), mouth (stay quiet), hands (calm), feet (quiet on floor), body (facing the speaker), brain (to think about what is being said), and heart (to care about what the person is saying).

Social Wonder: Thinking about what other people are interested in or how they feel and asking questions to gain more information from them about their interests, experiences, and thoughts.

Words Bumping: Another way to tell someone that they are interrupting.

Mood Meter

How are you feeling today?!

Place the following visual with different facial expressions/feelings on the refrigerator or a central location for the child and family to view. Have the child reference this visual on a daily basis to help determine how he or she is feeling and what mood he or she is in. Encourage the child to share those feelings and talk about why he or she is feeling that way. Be a model and do the same by telling the child how you are feeling and why.

Sample Conversation Cards

Tell me about the most fun part of your day today.	**What did you see or do at recess today?**
What do you think the party will be like this weekend?	**Tell me what your most favorite meal is.**
What is happening in your art class this week?	**Who would you spend time with this weekend if you could pick 3 people?**
If you could go anywhere on vacation, where would you go?	**Tell me about the most boring or difficult part of your day today.**
Tell me about the book you were reading in class today.	**What is something you are excited about tomorrow?**

Other ways to start open-ended questions include

1. Tell me what happened.
2. Why did you …?
3. How did you …?
4. What do you think?
5. Why do you think that happened?

6. Can you think of another way to think about that?
7. What can you tell me about …?
8. How did you do that?
9. Does that remind you of something else?
10. What do you think might happen next?

Wonder Questions

Use this visual to help the child come up with questions to ask other people. This can prompt the child to generate a question that keeps a conversation going and shows others that he or she is thinking about them.

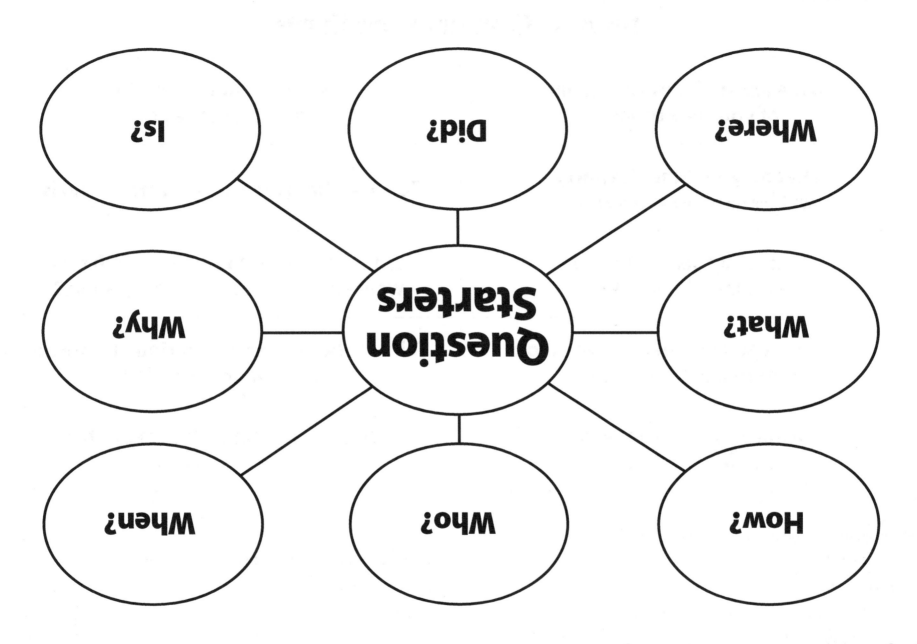

Question Starters

- Is?
- Did?
- Where?
- Why?
- What?
- When?
- Who?
- How?

Typical Dinner Schedule

Make dinner.	Set table.	Sit down, eat, and talk.	Clear table.	Clean up.

Get Ready, Do, Done Worksheet

1. Start with a picture of what a food item looks like when prepared and ready to eat (e.g., what does a ham sandwich look like when done?).
2. Figure out what steps you need to take to match the picture (DO).
3. What ingredients are needed to make the sandwich? (GET READY).

Now gather the ingredients, do the steps and when you are finished, look at it to make sure it matches the picture or what you hoped it would look like.

Eat it! (DONE). Great for building executive functioning skills!

Get Ready

What do I need?

- ☐ Ham
- ☐ Bread
- ☐ Cheese
- ☐ Lettuce
- ☐ Mayonnaise
- ☐ Knife
- ☐ Plate
- ☐ Other: _____

_____

1. Look at the Done picture.
2. List all ingredients or materials needed.

Do

List the steps:

Steps:
1. Get a plate.
2. Place two slices of bread on plate.
3. Use knife to spread mayo on one slice of bread.
4. Put cheese, lettuce, and ham on the same piece of bread.
5. Place other slice of bread on top of ham.
6. Cut sandwich in half.
7. Enjoy!

List what is needed to do with the ingredients or materials to complete the finished product/goal.

Done

Before starting, determine what the final product will look like.

Compare your finished product with the original picture or idea. Does it match?

Visual Schedule to Transition to Play Time

Hello   Sing   Play   Clean up   Snack   Good-bye

From *Peer Play and the Autism Spectrum: The Art of Guiding Children's Socialization and Imagination* by P. Wolfberg, 2003, Shawnee Mission, KS: AAPC Publishing, p. 68. Used with permission.

Sample Kid Jokes

Knock, knock!
Who's there?
Cash!
Cash who?
No thanks, but I'd like some peanuts!

Knock, knock!
Who's there?
Ken.
Ken who?
Ken I come in? It's freezing out here.

Sample Puns

- Time flies like an arrow. Fruit flies like a banana.
- I've been to the dentist many times so I know the drill.
- Without geometry, life is pointless.
- I went to a seafood disco last week .... and pulled a mussel.
- She had a photographic memory but never developed it.
- To write with a broken pencil is pointless.

Q: What did the triangle say to the circle?
A: You're so pointless.

Q: What did Bacon say to Tomato?
A: Lettuce get together!

Q: What do you call a sleeping bull?
A: A bulldozer!

Q: What do polar bears eat for lunch?
A: Ice berg-ers!

Q: How many skunks does it take to stink up a house?
A: A phew!

Q: Why do witches fly on brooms?
A: Because vacuum cleaners are too heavy!

Q: Which dog keeps the best time?
A: A watch dog.

Q: What do you call a snowman with a sun tan?
A: A puddle.

Q: What's black and white and makes a lot of noise?
A: A zebra with a drumkit.

5-Point Scale for Nighttime Routine

5 This made me feel awesome!!

4 This made me feel very happy!

3 This made me feel comfortable/OK.

2 This made me irritated.

1 This made me feel angry or mad.

Based on *The Incredible 5-Point Scale* by K. D. Buron and M. Curtis, 2012, Shawnee Mission, KS: AAPC Publishing. Used with permission.

Based on *The Incredible 5-Point Scale* by K. D. Buron and M. Curtis, 2012, Shawnee Mission, KS: AAPC Publishing. Used with permission.

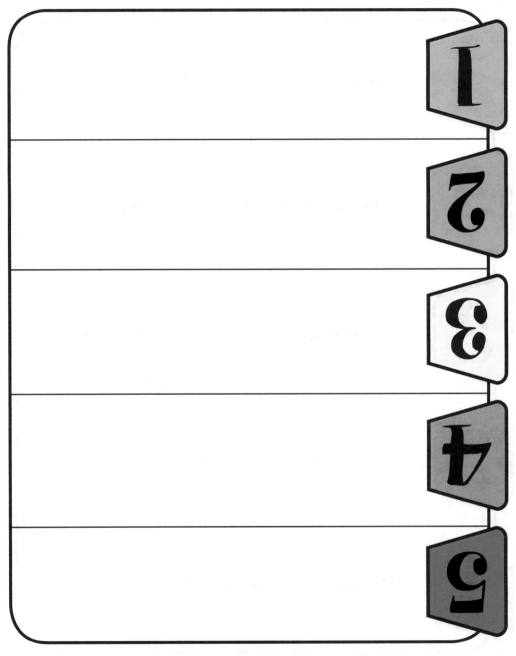

Blank 5-Point Scale

I Am Thankful Worksheet/Coupon

Use the following format to help the child write down things that he or she is thankful for. If writing is a challenge, have the child dictate to you or use photos or drawings. This can be done before bed, at the dinner table, or some other time when you have the child's attention. Helping the child be aware of the people and things that he or she is thankful for builds awareness of the good in life and creates positive thoughts. Post the sheet on the refrigerator to remind the child of the good in his or her life.

I am thankful for: *Because:*

1. _____   _____

2. _____   _____

3. _____   _____

4. _____   _____

5. _____   _____

Just for you!

This coupon is good for:

_____

           Thinking about you,

           _____

Steps for Brushing Teeth

1. Get toothbrush and toothpaste.	
2. Wet the toothbrush with water.	
3. Put toothpaste on toothbrush.	
4. Brush your teeth, each section (e.g., top & bottom, front & back, inside & outside) for at least 10 seconds, spitting toothpaste out as needed.	
5. Brush tongue.	
6. Rinse mouth with water.	
7. Put toothbrush and toothpaste away.	

Whole Body Listening Coloring Sheet

Whole body listening is a concept originally created by Susanne Poulette Truesdale in 1990. It was adapted and used by Sautter and Wilson in *Whole Body Listening Larry at School* and *Whole Body Listening Larry at Home*, 2011, San Jose, CA: Social Thinking Publishing. Used with permission.

Whole Body Listening Handout

1. Eyes = look at the person talking to you

2. Ears = both ears ready to hear

3. Mouth = quiet – no talking, humming, or making sounds

4. Hands = quiet in lap, pockets, or by your side

5. Feet = quiet on the floor

6. Body = faces the speaker

7. Brain = thinking about what is being said

8. Heart = caring about what the other person is saying

eyes watching   ears listening

mouth quiet   hands still

feet still   body facing speaker

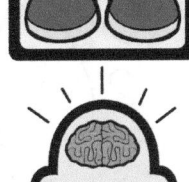

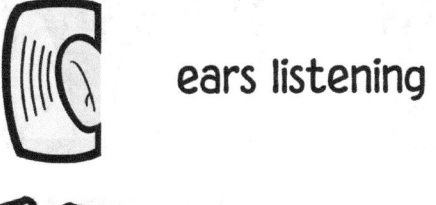

brain thinking   heart caring

Whole body listening is a concept originally created by Susanne Poulette Truesdale in 1990. It was adapted and used by Sautter and Wilson in *Whole Body Listening Larry at School* and *Whole Body Listening Larry at Home*, 2011, San Jose, CA: Social Thinking Publishing. Used with permission.

Sample "Would You Rather?" Questions

1. Would you rather always wear earmuffs or a nose plug?

2. Would you rather be a deep sea diver or an astronaut?

3. Would you rather be a dog named Killer or a cat named Fluffy?

4. Would you rather be a giant mouse or a tiny dinosaur?

5. Would you rather be able to hear any conversation or take back anything you say?

6. Would you rather be able to read everyone's mind all the time or always know their future?

7. Would you rather be able to stop time or fly?

8. Would you rather be an unknown minor league basketball player or a famous professional badminton star?

9. Would you rather be born with an elephant trunk or a giraffe neck?

10. Would you rather drink a cup of olive oil or a cup of pickle juice.

Sample Grocery List

Pantry/cupboards:		Refrigerator:		Bathroom:	
	Soup		Milk		Soap
	Syrup – Pancake		Butter		Shampoo & Conditioner
	Rice		Cheese		Mouth Wash
	Sugar – White		Lunch Meat		Toothpaste
	Tortilla Chips		Ketchup		Floss
	Bars – Granola Type		Mayo		Q Tips
	Honey		Jam – Strawberry	**Oops, I forgot:**	
	Coffee		Eggs		
	Cereal		Bread		
	Cinnamon	**Freezer:**			
	Salt		Hamburger Patties		
	Pepper		Ice Cream		
Produce:			Waffles – Frozen		
	Oranges		Pizza		
	Apples	**Household:**			
	Bananas		Dishwasher Detergent		
	Lettuce		Dish Soap	**Notes for next time:**	
	Tomatoes		Paper Plates		
			Napkins		
			Garbage Bags		
			Toilet Paper		

Social Autopsy Worksheet

When needed, sit down with the child and help him or her fill out this worksheet to help him or her understand how his or her behavior affected a social situation. Either you or the child can draw or write each step below.

Here's what was going on:	Here's what I did that caused a social error:	Here's what happened when I did that:	Here's what I should do to make things right:	Here's what I'll do next time:

Adapted from the work of Rick Lavoie (2005).

The Six Sides of Breathing

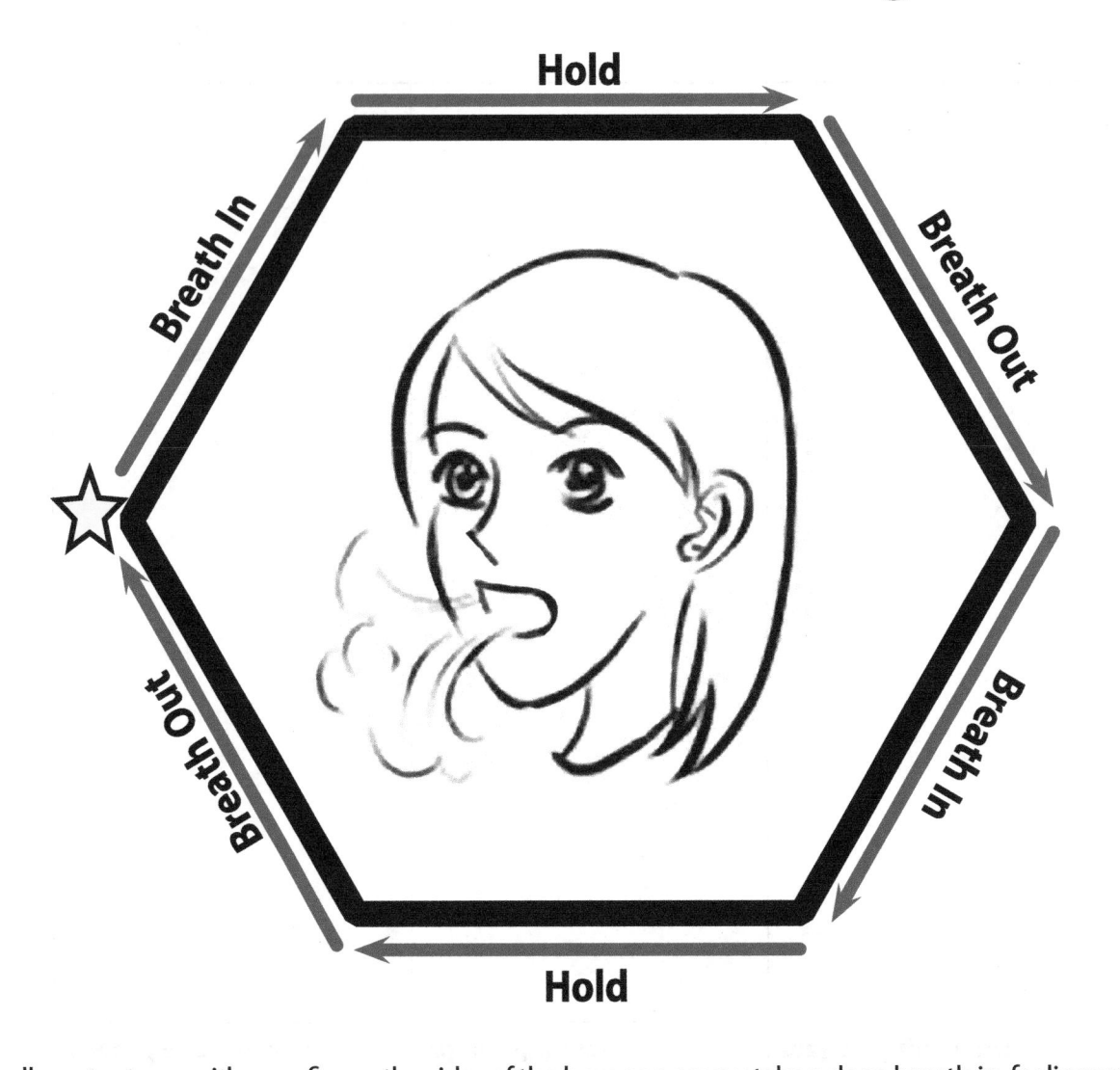

Starting at the yellow star trace with your finger the sides of the hexagon as you take a deep breath in, feeling your shoulders rise as the air fills you. Trace over the next side as you hold your breath for a moment. Slowly breathe out as you trace the third side of the hexagon. Continue tracing around the bottom three sides of the hexagon as you complete another deep breath. Continue The Six Sides of Breathing cycle until you feel calm and relaxed.

From L. Kuypers, *The Zones of Regulation*, 2008, San Jose, CA: Social Thinking Publishing, p. 118. Used with permission.

Sample Kid Tricks

Teach the child simple and fun skills to build confidence and use to break the ice when meeting new people or connecting with old ones. Below are some silly ideas to get started. Most will require demonstration and lots of practice. Once the child becomes a pro, encourage him or her to teach the skill to others.

Shuffling Cards – Split the deck of cards in half and hold half in each hand. Put your thumb on the edge of the cards that you want to merge into the other half of the deck. Put your ring and middle finger on the other end of the cards. Arch the cards in each hand and slowly pull your thumbs back, which will release the cards and file them into each other. With half of the deck merged into the other half, hold the position of your hands and bend the cards the other way so that they shuffle into each other and form a flat deck of cards.

Blowing Bubbles – Chew gum until it is soft. Make the gum flat and put it between the top of your mouth and the tongue. Hold the flattened gum with your jaw and stick your tongue slightly against the gum while blowing at the same time. Continue to blow until it is large enough to stop or it pops.

Skipping a Stone – Find a calm body of water and a flat, small stone. Hold the stone with your thumb and middle finger on either side of the edges, keeping the flat part up. Stand facing the water or to the side so that your body can twist toward the water then you throw. Aim and throw the stone very hard across the surface of the water with the flat part of the stone face up. Watch the stone dance and skip on the top of the water.

Doing Cartwheels – Make sure you have plenty of room and a flat, soft, safe space. Look for a straight line and spread your feet apart and put your arms straight above your head with your palms facing out and elbows straight. Turn one foot in the direction you want to go and bend over sideways while kicking your legs off the ground and into the air. Keep your eyes looking at your hands and where your feet will land and place your feet firmly on the ground. It should go hand, hand, foot, foot in that order on the ground.

Juggling – Get three beanbags or balls that do not bounce. Practice passing one ball from one hand to the other and throwing one ball in the air and catching it with the same hand. Practice "scooping," which is a simple shallow scoop or dip that you do with your hand before tossing the ball in the air. Practice tossing with two balls, throwing them in the air and catching them. When the first ball is at the peak of the arc, toss the next one, catching them as they fall. When comfortable with this, add a third ball. Throw the balls in the air when they are at the peak of the arc, always ready with another ball to throw up.

Jokes – Get a joke book or go online to look up age appropriate jokes. Make sure you pick a joke that is appropriate for the audience, especially for the age and the interest of the people you are telling it to. If you tell a joke that is topic specific or that is too complicated for the age of the listener, it won't be funny. Practice the joke by yourself or with a family member. Practice setting it up (laying the foundation) and making a strong punchline (the funny part). If the listener doesn't get it or think it's funny, try to explain it so they join in the laughter/humor.

Fun With Language – Teach your child a made up language such as pig Latin, a code language or even a tongue twister that they can teach to other children such as "She sells seashells on the seashore".

Whistling – Shape the lips as if you were going to make the sound "ooh" or in a small circle (e.g., pucker lips). Curl the tongue slightly on each edge and press it against the roof of the mouth. Blow a steady, smooth stream of air through the opening of the tongue and lips. Adjust lips and tongue position until sound comes out as a whistling noise.

Funny Facts – Have your child research funny, interesting, or odd facts to share with others, such as "It's impossible to sneeze with your eyes open" or "Rabbits and parrots can see behind themselves without even moving their heads!". They can practice telling these to the family first and then branch out to their peers when ready. Help them use phrases such as "did you know?"… or "I just learned something interesting, do you want to know, too?"

Special Interests and Knowledge – For kids who have a special interest such as geography, trains, number knowledge or sports information, have them practice sharing that information with their peers in a way that makes other people interested. For example, if they know a lot about geography or sports, they can have a peer quiz them about state capitals or which sports teams play in different states.

Sample Social Narrative

Use this or a similar story to help the child know what is going to happen when going to the beach.

This vacation I will be spending time at the beach. I will bring towels and chairs to sit on and food to eat. It is usually sunny at the beach, so I will need my sunglasses and sunscreen.

I will play in the sand and in the water. If there are other kids playing in the sand or water, I can ask them to play with me. Maybe we can build a sand castle together. I will share my sand toys with the other kids.

I will try not to get sand on other people when they are lying on their towels or in the food.

I will be careful when I am in the ocean and stay with an adult at all times when I am in the water. The sand might be hot and the ocean might be cold.

Going to the beach is a fun and relaxing thing to do.

Interest Inventory for Reinforcement Menu

Ask the child to put a check next to at least 5 items/activities that he or she would most like to earn at home. Add items or change the list to make it specific for the child. (Read the list to non-readers or use photos or visuals and help them mark the items they select.)

_____1.　Hug, high five, or verbal praise

_____2.　Food treat (can be specific here)

_____3.　Coloring/drawing

_____4.　Computer time, video games, TV

_____5.　Play with friends

_____6.　Stickers

_____7.　Going for a walk

_____8.　Play with favorite toy (can be specific; Legos®, puzzles, train, Barbies®)

_____9.　Reading time

_____10.　Time with adult

_____11.　Written note about good behavior on refrigerator

Useful WebSites

Social and Self-Regulation

- The Alert Program® & How Does Your Engine Run?
  www.alertprogram.com
- Brain Gym®
  www.brainygym.org
- Center on the Social and Emotional Foundations for Early Learning (CSEFEL)
  http://csefel.vanderbilt.edu/
- Comic Strip Conversations/Social Stories and More
  www.thegraycenter.org
- The Explosive Child
  www.explosivechild.com
- The Incredible 5-Point Scale
  www.5pointscale.com
- Interactive Teaching Tool for Social Skills
  http://www.playtimewithzeebu.com/about/
- No Bully
  www.nobully.com
- Online Asperger Syndrome Information & Support (OASIS)
  www.aspergersyndrome.org
- The SCERTS® Model, Education Approach for Children With Autism Spectrum Disorders
  www.scerts.com
- Social and Emotional Skills Sharing Site
  www.jillkuzma.wordpress.com
- Social-Emotional Animals and Curriculum
  http://www.kimochis.com/
- Social Thinking, Michelle Garcia Winner
  www.socialthinking.com
- Software for Social Skills
  www.socialskillbuilder.com
- Tony Attwood, Asperger's Syndrome Resources
  www.tonyattwood.com.au
- The Zones of Regulation®
  www.zonesofregulation.com

Speech and Language

- American Speech and Language Association
  www.asha.org
- Information About Speech-Language Development
  www.ican.org.uk
- Information on Hearing Impairments
  www.listen-up.org
- Information for Parents to Infuse Language at Home
  www.speech-language-development.com
- Selective Mutism
  www.selectivemutism.org

Early Intervention

- The Hanen Centre
  www.hanen.org

- Parent Pals
  www.parentpals.com

- Pathways Awareness Foundation
  www.pathwaysawareness.org

- DIR/Floortime
  http://www.icdl.com/dirFloortime/overview/

Sensory Processing and Occupational Therapy

- The American Occupational Therapy Association
  www.aota.org

- Information on Sensory Processing Disorder
  www.sensory-processing-disorder.com

- Recognizing & Coping with Sensory Processing Disorder
  www.out-of-sync-child.com

Autism Spectrum Disorders

- Treatment Tips for Children with Autism Spectrum Disorders
  www.autismtreatment.info
  www.thebolickhouse.com

Learning Disabilities

- LD Online
  www.ldonline.org

- National Center for Learning Disabilities
  www.ncld.org

- NLD on the Web
  www.nldontheweb.org

Executive Functioning and ADD/ADHD

- Children & Adults with ADHD
  www.chadd.org

- Diagnosis and Treatment of ADHD
  www.help4adhd.org/en/treatment

- Executive Function Therapy
  www.cognitiveconnectionstherapy.com

- Information Sheets about ADHD
  www.help4adhd.org/en/about/wwk

- The M.I.N.D. Institute
  www.mindinstitute.org

Suggested Extracurricular Social Activities
(After School and on Weekends)

Physical/Sports Interests

Sports and board games are not just about winning and losing. Although those are important skills to learn to manage gracefully, children learn many other skills through play, such as problem solving, negotiating, turn-taking, conflict resolution, patience, sportsmanship, how to follow the rules, and how to relate to others. Below are some suggestions for games and sports the child might enjoy. Always keep the child's interests and skills in mind. If you opt for a team sport, investigate the coach's style and expectations before getting the child involved. Have the child watch someone else playing the game or sport to build interest, awareness, and confidence before jumping in.

To start, consider sports/recreational activities that don't create excessive pressure to perform for the team, including

- Swimming
- Karate
- Tennis
- Skiing

When ready, choose sports that involve practicing teamwork and sportsmanship, including

- Swim team
- Track and field
- Soccer
- Baseball
- Basketball

Academic Interests

For children who are more academically driven or have an artistic/creative side, use these interests and skills to help incorporate social participation. Academic group work and study groups can bring children together to practice social interaction. Clubs, events, or activities that include others are great ways to get involved and practice working with others.

- Chess
- Book club
- Science club
- Computer club
- Debate team
- Journalism

Creative Interests

- Art
- Pottery
- Drama
- Music/band
- Puzzles with other people
- Wii® sports with others
- Boy/Girl Scouts
- Building Legos® or other construction

Other

- Card games that involve other people (not solitaire)
- Pokémon® or other trading cards with friends
- Board games

Note about special interests (trains, Legos®, Star Wars®, bugs, etc.): Try to find a way to incorporate the child's special interests into a social event. For example, have the child build a model train with another student in an art class or on a play date.

Recommended Movies/DVDs

- *Playtime With Zeebu* (Thought Bubble Productions)

- *Wallace and Gromit* (National Film and Television School, Aardman Animations, DreamWorks, DreamWorks Animation)

- *The Pink Panther*, rated PG (Sony Pictures Home Entertainment)

- *Charlie Brown* movies or TV specials by Charles Schultz

- *Finding Nemo*, rated G (Walt Disney Studios Home Entertainment 2003)

- *Toy Story*, rated G (Pixar Animation Studios)

- *Bean* and *Mr. Bean's Holiday*, rated PG 13 (Working Title Films)

- Claymation movies – many titles and companies

- *Winnie the Pooh* movies, rated G (Disney)

Recommended Games

The following are examples of games for improving all areas of language, including social skills. Playing games with the child also helps with turn taking, sharing, flexibility, problem solving, and sportsmanship. Games can be modified depending on the child's needs. Start slowly with just you and the child. Model and reinforce positive social interactions and skills. When the child is comfortable playing with you, begin to add siblings or other children to practice what the child has learned.

Board and Card Games

- *Apples to Apples*® – Mattel
- *Battleship*® – Milton Bradley
- *Blurt*® – made by Blurt
- *Bubble Brain*® – Patch Products
- *Cranium Cadoo*® – Cranium, Inc.
- *Cranium Whoonu*® – Cranium, Inc.
- *Emotional Bingo*® – Active Parenting Publishers
- *Go Fish*® and *Kings*® (card games)
- *Guess Where*® – Hasbro, Milton Bradley and others

- *Guess Who*® – Hasbro, Milton Bradley and others
- *Guesstures*® – Milton Bradley
- *Hedbanz*® – Spin Master Games
- *I Spy Preschool Game*® – Briarpatch
- *Kids on Stage*® – Kids on Stage, Inc.
- *Mad Chatter*® – Hersch & Co.
- *Mad Libs*® – Price, Stern, Sloan
- *Outburst Junior*® – Parker Brothers
- *Pictionary and Pictionary Jr.*® – Hasbro

- *Red Light, Green Light*® – Tara Toy Corp.
- *Scattergories*® – Hasbro
- *Should I or Should I Not*® – Social Thinking
- *Taboo and Taboo Junior*® – Hasbro
- *Twister*® – Milton Bradley
- *Would You Rather?*® – Zobmondo
- *You Gotta Be Kidding*® – Zobmondo

Other Family Games

- Charades
- Follow the leader

- Freeze dance
- Hide and seek

- Musical chairs
- Scavenger hunts

- "Simon Says …"

Setting up Successful Play Dates

- Make sure the child is ready and willing to have a play date. Don't force anything or put the child in a situation that is too challenging, such as going swimming if the child does not know how to swim. It is important to make sure it is a successful and rewarding experience for everybody involved.

- Start at a park or neutral place. Sometimes just hanging out on the playground after school is a great start. It can be hard for some kids to understand what having a guest means and how to share or welcome a guest.

- Have a play date at your home before sending the child to a friend's house.

- Keep it short and limit the amount of children at one given time.

- Pick a good time. Make sure the child is well rested, healthy, and that the date is absent of new transitions and/or changes. Avoid nap times, difficult times in the day for the child, periods after a holiday or vacation when schedules/routines have changed.

- Pick well-matched play partners – this significantly influences the process. Generally, select children who are younger or a little older, or familiar kids that the child prefers. Do not include siblings at first because the playmate/guest might prefer playing with the sibling.

- Try to schedule play dates on a regular basis – at a park, another person's house or your house for an after school snack.

- Plan ahead. Arrange for preferred, familiar games or activities (e.g., art, hide-and-seek, duck, duck goose). Sharing and trading can be hard at first, so prepare the child by talking to him about what a guest is and

---

- what is *expected* of both the host and the guest. Talk about the rules with both of the children at the start of the play date. Remove special toys and have two toys for each activity.

- Get involved. Don't just let them play by themselves and hope for the best. Change activities when needed, help with sharing and negotiating and facilitating play together, but don't dominate or fill in for the child. The idea is to break the ice, reinforce, and facilitate without taking control. Back off as soon as you can.

- Make the last 15 minutes the most fun (e.g., snack or special activity) as this is what the children will remember best. Recap the play date and discuss what went well and what didn't.

- Be a play date yourself. This is a good way to figure out what areas the child needs help in and to identify her strengths (if she struggles with puzzles, leave them out of play dates with kids, etc.). Don't forget to model *expected* social behavior yourself – imitation is HUGE! Narrate your feelings, thoughts, and actions.

- If the child isn't ready for other children, a furry friend or pet can be less threatening and a good introduction to being social. For example, have the child play with the dog by throwing a ball to him. This back-and-forth interaction can be a start to interacting more with other people.

- Don't expect too much too early. If the child is younger it is developmentally appropriate to play mostly side-by-side and imitate rather than interact. Too much pressure can cause stress on both the child and the play date.

RELATED BOOKS FROM AAPC

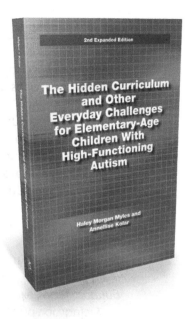

Diary of a Social Detective
Real-Life Tales of Mystery, Intrigue and Interpersonal Adventure

by Jeffrey E. Jessum, PhD

ISBN 9781934575710 | Code 9063 | Price: $20.00
Also available as an ebook!

Social Rules for Kids
The Top 100 Social Rules Kids Need to Succeed

by Sue Diamond, MA, CCC

ISBN 9781934575840 | Code 9067 | Price: $20.00
Also available as an ebook!

The Hidden Curriculum and Other Everyday Challenges for Elementary-Age Children With High-Functioning Autism

by Haley Morgan Myles and Annellise Kolar

ISBN 9781937473105 | Code 9917 | Price: $15.00

To order and for more information, visit www.aapcpublishing.net

More Advance Praise ...

"Elizabeth Sautter has written a book that gives parents, teachers, and other important individuals in children's lives the tools they need to facilitate social growth. *Make Social Learning Stick!* incorporates the work of a small community of scholars and hands-on practitioners who specialize in developing communication and self-regulation skills in children. As a parent of a child who was slow to develop self-regulation and perspective-taking skills, I can verify that the guidelines and examples provided in this book are effective. The decision to make learning fun through play, lay out the hidden rules for various situations, and give parents meaningful and constructive language, allows them not only to be mentors for their children with social difficulties but also to gently instruct the community of people who care for their children on how to be more encouraging and effective role-models. I recommend this book for anyone who has children, works with children, or cares about and wants to help children progress in their social learning."

— Hilary R. Altman, PhD, chair, Communication, Merritt College

"*Make Social Learning Stick!* is a must-have resource for parents and therapists wanting to enhance children's social emotional development around the home and community. By laying out simple activities, strategies, and vocabulary that can be interwoven into daily activities to support children in learning fundamental social skills, *Make Social Learning Stick!* provides an important bridge between skills a child may be learning at school or therapy and the home. I will be recommending this book to families of clients I treat, as well as integrating the fun, playful ideas into my own home with my children."

— Leah Kuypers, MA Ed, OTR/L, occupational therapist, consultant; author of *The Zones of Regulation*

"*Make Social Learning Stick!* is a delightful book that includes child- and family-centered tools and techniques for meeting the unique social communication needs of diverse learners on the autism spectrum. This is a go-to resource for applying effective, user-friendly practices across natural settings and contexts throughout the child's day at home, at school, and in the community. I am excited to share this with my students and the many families we serve around the world."

— Pamela Wolfberg, PhD, San Francisco State University and Autism Institute on Peer Socialization and Play

"*Make Social Learning Stick!* is a treasure trove of practical suggestions intended to help children with social challenges. Parents, therapists, and teachers will find themselves dipping into this indispensable book on a regular basis for effective ideas. All children will benefit from Sautter's approach to teachable moments."

— Rebecca Schwartz, PhD, clinical psychologist, private practice, San Francisco Center for Psychoanalysis

APC PUBLISHING

P.O. Box 23173
Shawnee Mission, Kansas 66283-0173
www.aapcpublishing.net